CALABASH

A Guide to the History, Culture,
and Art of African Americans
in Seattle and King County,
Washington

Esther Hall Mumford

Ananse Press
Seattle

Mumford, Esther Hall
CALABASH
A Guide to the History, Culture, and Art of African
Americans in Seattle and King County, Washington
ISBN 0-9605670-7-0

Printed in the United States of America

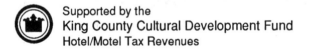

Supported by the
King County Cultural Development Fund
Hotel/Motel Tax Revenues

Book design by Sea-Hill Press

Contents

Office of the Mayor
City of Seattle

Norman B. Rice, Mayor

July 1992

Esther Hall Mumford
Ananse Press
P.O. Box 22565
Seattle, Washington 98122

Dear Ms. Mumford:

As Mayor of the City of Seattle, I am happy to extend my support and best wishes to your new guidebook, *CALABASH: A Guide to the History, Culture and Art of African Americans in Seattle and King County, Washington.*

African Americans have made contributions to the cultural, economic, artistic, social and religious life of our community. Your new guide will highlight these valuable contributions and act as a beacon for people, especially youth, who are not aware of the multitude of endeavors African Americans have been involved in.

CALABASH will be an important resource, not just for African Americans, but for everyone who wants to know more about the richness and beauty provided by the diversity of the Puget Sound area.

On behalf of the people of Seattle, congratulations on the publication of this wonderful guidebook.

Sincerely,

Norman B. Rice

King County Executive
TIM HILL

King County Courthouse
516 Third Avenue   Room 400
Seattle, Washington 98104-3271

(206) 296-4040
FAX: **(206) 296-0194**

July 29, 1992

I am delighted to introduce *CALABASH: A Guide to the History, Culture and Art of African Americans in Seattle and King County, Washington* by Esther Hall Mumford. Ms. Mumford is an accomplished author and a noted historian. She has been honored with a number of awards, including the State Centennial Commission's "Living Historical Treasure Award" in 1989.

This guide, published under a grant from King County's Cultural Development Fund, is a valuable introduction to the many contributions of citizens of African American heritage to the cultural life of King County. It speaks well of the County's continued commitment to the preservation and celebration of our region's cultural diversity.

King County is the leading tourism destination in Washington State and the Pacific Northwest. My hope is that visitors and residents alike will find in this guide a wealth of information about the African American Community which will help them to explore and to enjoy these aspects of King County's rich cultural landscape.

Sincerely,

Tim Hill
King County Executive

Acknowledgements

Many people assisted the writing of this book by sharing their recollections, papers, photographs and referrals. They are: Mary Moore, Jacqueline Cotton, Juanita Proctor, Lora Chiora Dye, Leon Bridges, The Rev. Robert Hayes, Shirley Glass, Renee Miller, Thelma McAdoo, Barbara Pool, Michael Ziegler, Mark Wilson, Janet Batiste, Janice Cook, The Rev. M. E. Hale, Patti Allen, Lisa Harris, Maurice Scott, Sheree Sparks, Robert Otis, Jones Clavier Academy, Dr. Anita Connell, Stanley Friendship, George Monroe, William Southern, Lillian Gideon, Monad, The Rev. Wilbur Vincent, Alexander Conley, Carrolle Fair Perry, Dr. Meredith Matthews, Starms Washington, Sen. Dwight Pelz's Office, Representative Jim McDermott's Office, Sara Oliver Jackson, Suzanne Albright, Antioch Bible Church, Theodosia Young, Gloria McCoy, Dior Seck, Beverly Mendheim, Ali Scego, Marie Roston, Beverly Lucas, Office of Chief Claude Harris, Chief Al Lee, Frank Wilkins, Councilwoman Sherry Harris, Vickie Hanson, Larry Clarke, Connie Cameron, Sam Cameron, Mel Streeter, Lauri Wilson, Donald King, Abba Haddis Gedey, Al Poole, Leslie Main, Rhonda Gossett, Maryee Richardson Johnson, Dr. John German, Dr. Donald Phelps, Janet Austin, Ben Franklin, Ron and Iris Franklin, Bill and Ceta Wright, Alice Nelson, Eleanor and Rudolph Hill, Barbara Thomas, Florence Baker-Wood, James W. and Janie Washington, Rubi Williams, Joe Jones, Susan Cayton Woodson, Charlena Mace, Oneida Hall Gallerson, First African Methodist Church, Carletta Wilson, Carole Williams, B. F. Day Parent Volunteers, Diane Hepfer, Zola Mumford, Carl and Ann Steiert, Rilla Allen, Barbara Green, Joseph Warner, Njambi Gishuru, Linda Brown, Pat Lacey, Sandra Kirk Roston, Maxine Pitter Haynes, Ernestine Chatman, Roberta Byrd Barr, Irene Grayson, Ron Douglass, Charles Lewis, Hayward Roberts, Ora Avis Dennis, Marjorie Pitter King, Paul de Barros, Thomas Gayton, Sid White, Stan Greene, Ruby Martin, Emily Larkins, Helen Grayson and Shirley Phelps.

I am indebted to several research sources: Mike Saunders of the King County Regional Branch, Washington State Archives; Scott Cline, City of Seattle Municipal Archives; Public Information Office, Bellevue Public Schools; Seattle Public Library Magazines, Newspapers and Government Publications Department; City of Sea-Tac Planning and Community Development Office; the U. S. Census Bureau; and Francine Seder Gallery. Many thanks to Greg and Cindy Sharp of Sea-Hill Press for their patient shepherding of this book from its early, rough stages through to the finished product.

A repeated thanks to my mentor, Tim Frederick, is always in order. Bob Pickens, of the People's Photography Studio in Tacoma, turned up at the door to offer photographs, and even more importantly, to ask what he could do to help. Some of his photographs of sites and artwork included here are the result. Newcastle Historical society members, Oliver and Mary Jo Rouse spent the better part of an early autumn afternoon showing my husband, Don, and me the Newcastle Cemetery and sharing the interment record they here painstakingly compiled. Charles Payton, Community Museum Advisor and best friend to small museums and independent researchers, was continuously helpful in providing maps, information, and telephone numbers for county contacts. Bill and Ceta Wright sent material on golf club discrimination and, in a long telephone call from Los Angeles, answered many questions regarding his and his parents' personal experiences in their fight for equality in that sport.

The friendship and support of Priscilla Kirk dates to 1975 when I first met her during the Washington State Oral History project. She was my guide in her old Green Lake neighborhood. Her death in November eclipsed my plan to return in triumph to show her the former Ray home which, because of street changes and my unfamiliarity with the area as a driver, we had been unable to find during an earlier exploration.

A grant from the King County Cultural Development Fund Hotel/Motel Tax Revenue made possible the printing of this guidebook. The maps, with some alterations, are reprinted with the permission of US WEST DIRECT, publishers of the WHITE and YELLOW PAGES.

Several people supported the work by ordering advance copies of the book. They are: Lawrence Clarke, Ed and Millie Russell, Mary Henry, Horace Foxall, Dr. Michael and Carol Washington, Judge Charles Stokes, Mildred Andrews, Alfred Poole, Ora Avis Dennis, Sara D. Kaplan, Maxine Pitter Haynes, Pauline S. Hill, Dr. Rosalind Woodhouse, Gwendolyn Townsend, and the Rev. Wilbur Vincent. An additional gift from Horace Foxall helped to defray some of the miscellaneous expenses.

Two persons were indispensable to me in completing this book:

Denice Johnson Hunt, upon learning of my effort to write the book, was unstinting in her encouragement. She read the first draft, offered suggestions, provided maps of the city for possible inclusion, and co-edited the book.

My husband, Donald Emerson Mumford, has long been my most valuable ally in my endeavors. Not only has he served in the traditional role of bringing home the bacon, but he has rarely complained when it was late or unprepared, while I read, researched and rummaged around for unexplored places to include in the book. Time and again he accompanied me around the county to make photographs of many of the places recorded in this book. His love and patience makes my work possible.

ESTHER HALL MUMFORD
December 1992, Seattle, Washington

Preface

African Americans in King County have welcomed visitors since the late 1850s when Manuel Lopes rented beds to overnight guests and newcomers to Seattle.

Each day more than 10,000 cars pass 23rd Avenue and Yesler Way, one of the areas in Seattle with a concentration of African American residents. Most of the passersby barely take notice of the neighborhood. Indeed, many of the newer residents of this and other communities are unaware of the history of much that they see.

This guide is intended to acquaint county residents and visitors with some of the more easily accessible landmarks of African American history. These include works of art and historical and cultural sites which have been passed or driven by, for years while their existence, significance or association with African Americans in King County over the past century and a half has gone unnoted. This book provides information to give the user a sense of the creators and participants, the places and the activities associated with them. It will help to increase our understanding of the communities in which we live, and enhance visitors' appreciation for the places they see.

Use it to while away a weekend at a festival, get in shape with Afroaerobics, savor award-winning food, visit a church with African-inspired architecture, and visit a quiet century-old cemetery. Parents and teachers may find it a handy resource for use with children. Use it to retrace the steps of coal miners of the 1890s, look up at a gigantic mural, or down at a life-sized carved fish on a sidewalk. You may view an African drummer in stone or hear a live one in concert.

Over 4,000 miles in King County are traversed by Metro. Travel by bus brings the nondriver within walking distance of the sites or activities throughout the county.

Except for private homes and corporations, most of the art and sites included here are accessible to public viewers. They are marked on the maps accompanying each section. The residences cited here are marked by a symbol (∧) and are not open for visits. They are no longer occupied by the original history-makers or their families. Security measures dictated omission of homes of such African American trailblazers as Seattle Mayor Norman Rice and Washington State Supreme Court Justice Charles Z. Smith. While some of the sites have specific hours, most can be enjoyed at the visitor's convenience. In some areas a "windshield tour" may suffice; in others you will not be satisfied until you walk around, get up close, and perhaps touch some of the objects of interest, sample the food, or visit the event.

The book begins with an exploration of the northwest side of the county, moving first through that part of Seattle west of Interstate-5 to Federal Way in the southwest. For the areas east of Lake Washington the guide provides more of a historical background, tracing the growth and dispersal of the African American population, than an exploration of present day sites to visit.

From large outdoor earthworks to small utilitarian objects, King County is rich in art and, while not old by the standards of eastern states, it is rich in history. African Americans have been part of that history, and have contributed to the county's growth and development since the early days of settlement.

In African culture the calabash is important for sustenance and storing food, as musical instruments, and for a variety of other practical or daily purposes. In the title it is used in the sense of South African poet Amelia Blossom Pegram's description of the African Way as "cooking in a big pot," so that there is enough for everyone who may drop by. From King County's African American population there is food, music, art, history and architecture for all who stop and take the time to learn about them and enjoy them.

In memory of
Priscilla Maunder Kirk,
1898-1992

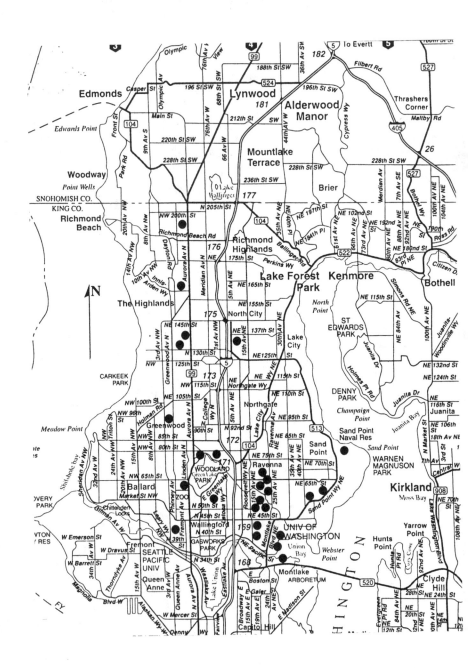

1.
North End

Beyond Green Lake

African Americans are scarcely mentioned in extant sources about the northern part of the county. Most settled in the central and southeastern areas, but through the years a few have lived and worked near Green Lake and beyond. In the 1970s, an elderly Shoreline resident mentioned in *Shoreline Memories* (Shoreline Historical Society) a **Mrs. Hunt**, a former slave, who lived at Richmond Beach with her Caucasian husband and worked as a nurse in the area earlier this century. Since World War II, there has been more substantial evidence of African American presence or involvement with the area.

In 1958, architect **Benjamin McAdoo** designed the Richmond Highlands Baptist Church, *19350 Firlands Way N.*, which has since been remodelled. It was a smaller version of the New Hope Baptist Church in Seattle's Central Area which he designed in 1951.

Present-day residents contribute to the progress of the county in many ways. Lake Forest Park resident, **Joseph Ward**, was appointed to the King County Arts Commission in 1987. Ward, a vice-president at First Interstate Bank, is active in regional and national family services organizations. He is a former member of the Metropolitan Arts Commission of Portland.

At Shoreline Community College, *16101 Greenwood Avenue N.*, *546-4101*, rooms 1302-1303 of the 1300 Building were renamed the **Sam Kelly Lecture Hall** in 1980 to honor **Dr. Samuel Kelly** who was Assistant to the President for Minority Student Affairs at the college prior to his 1970 appointment as vice-president for minority affairs at the University of Washington. Kelly served on the college's Board of Trustees in the 1980s. He and sociology professor **Larry Clarke** were largely responsible for the establishment of Shoreline's Ethnic Studies Department, the first such college department in the state. Clarke initiated a number of sociology courses at the college dealing with ethnic diversity and a two quarter African American history course.

Robert Colbert became the first person in the state to head such a department when it was established in 1970. Shoreline is the only community college in the state which requires five hours of what is now called Inter-American Studies towards an associate degree.

One of the great success stories of King County residents is that of **William McIntosh of North Seattle Chrysler Plymouth**, *13733 Aurora Avenue N.* In just four years, beginning in 1986, he resuscitated a bankrupt car dealership, and turned it into one of the top Chrysler-Plymouth outlets in the country. McIntosh, a graduate of the University of Minnesota, is sole proprietor of one of the county's largest African American businesses, and has seventy employees.

As one of the co-chairs of the **Martin Luther King Memorial Committee** he helped to revitalize a flagging effort. He was one of the signers of the guarantee note pledging to repay King County's $25,000 contribution should the memorial not be completed within a specified time.

The Jackson Park Golf Course, *1000 NE 135th*, is just a few minutes drive to the east. The golf club was one of the first two in Seattle to accept an African American member, when **Fay Kimbrough** was admitted to the women's club in 1958. (The other club was West Seattle Women's Club.)

If you don't golf, you may want to try bingo. The income generated by **Aurora Bingo,** *13202 Aurora N.*, is the chief source of income for the **Central Area Youth Association,** sponsor of a variety of programs for children of low-income families. This activity initially began in a former supermarket at 23rd Avenue and Union Street.

When **Sherry Harris,** Seattle's first African American City Council-woman, declared her candidacy, and listed as part of her resume her previous service as president of the Maple Leaf Community Club, many people wondered where Maple Leaf was. It was not unknown to preceding generations, however.

The **Sons of Enterprise** held the county's first "**Juneteenth**" celebration in 1890 in Kent, followed the next year by a July event attended by about 150 people who rode a chartered train to Maple Leaf for an all-day picnic. Harris, a former engineer

Sherry Harris,
first African American woman elected to
the Seattle City Council.

for US West Communications, moved to Seattle in 1978. She holds a B.S. in Ergonomic Design and a Masters of Business Administration. Postal clerk Richard Roots and his wife Sarah, a dermatologist, lived in the area during the 1920s.

Viacom Community Television, *8914 Roosevelt Way NE*, one of three public access stations in the county, is in Maple Leaf. Several programs on African American social and cultural issues are produced here.

In the Greenwood Area the tiny, pleasant Koinonia Smokehouse, *8733 Greenwood Avenue N.*, *781-8678*, a restaurant with a wallpaper border which bears the New Testament inscription "the fruit of the spirit is love, joy, peace," features barbecue. The menu includes a *smoked* potato. Breakfast is served all day. The restaurant's own "Plobbler" (sweet potato and peach cobbler) is offered seasonally. Be sure to try the bacon muffin. In addition to the food, the restaurant hosts Christian music and singing on Friday and Saturday nights. A women's prayer group, LOVE, meets there Thursday evenings at 7pm. Senior citizens receive twenty percent discount every Tuesday. *Hours are Tuesday-Friday 11am-4pm, Saturday, 10am-5pm. Closed Sunday.*

Francine Seders Gallery, *6701 Greenwood Avenue N.*, *782-0355*, represents artists Marita Dingus, Phillip Lewis, Barbara Thomas, Jacob Lawrence and his wife, former King County Arts Commissioner, Gwen Knight Lawrence. A group show in February of 1988 featured their work in addition to that of other African American artists of renown.

Woodland Park

Woodland Park was the favored site of the annual Sunday School Picnic which was first held in 1891 at Lake Washington by the African Methodist Episcopal Church. In the following years, the Baptists and Presbyterians joined in sponsoring the outing. Seattle resident Muriel Pollard remembers the picnic in the 1920s: "Sunday School picnics were a big thing. The churches would furnish ice cream for the children and coffee for the adults, and everybody brought their lunch. We'd play games and run races. Some...went down to swim in Green Lake. It was something that we all looked forward to. It was one of the big events of the year."

The Poncho Theater at the Woodland Park Zoo, *50th and Fremont*, is the home of the Seattle Children's Theater which has featured plays with African American themes and actors. A play on Harriet Tubman by poet, novelist, and professor of English, Colleen McElroy premiered here. In 1983 McElroy became the first female of African descent to receive appointment as a full professor at the University of Washington. Her publications include five books of poetry, and one of short stories. *The Former One-on-One Basketball Champion*, played at the Poncho in 1990. It starred **Bill Russell**, former NBA player, who became coach and general manager of the Seattle Supersonics basketball team in 1973. The history-based musical collage *Black Stage Views*, written by members of the original company, opened at the Bathhouse Theater, *7312 West Green Lake Drive N.*, *524-9108*, in 1990 and toured county stages and schools.

In the **African Savannah** area of the zoo one of the large rock viewpoints bears a memorial plaque to **Jimi Hendrix**, the great pioneer rock guitarist. The plaque was funded by world-wide donations to KZOK Radio. *Entrance and parking at North 50th Street and Fremont Avenue, 684-4800. Parking, $1.00 for four hours; entrance fees, $5.00 for adults, $2.75 for school age children.* Bring binoculars, and stay and visit the rest of the zoo.

The earliest African American landowner in the north end was **William Hedges** who, in 1865, traded one hundred and twenty feet of a lot at the northwest corner of Fourth Avenue South, facing on Washington Street, for forty-seven acres in the Green Lake District. (The exact location of this property is not known due to the original holder's failure to register the transfer of the property at the county assessor's office.) Hedges's possession of it is mentioned in a local newspaper at the time of his death when the entire parcel was sold at auction for $265! The Fourth Avenue property was a subject of dispute in an 1895 court case where Hedges's Green Lake property was also mentioned.

African Americans have resided in the Green Lake area since at least the turn of the century. Lloyd Ray, a stonecutter, and his wife, **Emma**, moved to Seattle from Kansas City when he sought employment in the rebuilding of the city following the Great Fire of 1889. His wife, Emma Ray, was a founding member of the **First African Methodist Episcopal Church** and organizer of the **Frances Harper Union**, the African American branch of the Woman's Christian Temperance Union in the 1890s. At the turn of the century the Rays operated a Pioneer Square mission to minister to gold miners returning from the Yukon and Alaska.

Emma Ray's 1926 autobiography, *Twice Bought, Twice Ransomed*, describes the early days of the African Methodist Church and some aspects of the 1890s' African American population. To see their house, which Lloyd Ray built mostly by himself, leave East Green Lake *Drive* N. and travel to *7526 Sunnyside N.* (∿). The stone retaining wall that Lloyd Ray erected bears witness to his skill.

In 1901, **George** and **Sadie Maunder** purchased a quarter of a block which included *2127 North 59th and Kensington Place* (∿). Their family home, with slight exterior modification, still stands today. Mr. Maunder was an Irishman from County Cork, Ireland who met and married Sadie Heights, an African Canadian, in Nanaimo, British Columbia, Canada, where their first child, George, was born. The house was sold by the Maunder family in 1950.

In the same neighborhood, at *2320 North 53rd* (∧), is the birthplace of the late ballerina and modern dance teacher, Syvilla Fort, daughter of mail carrier John Fort and his wife, Mildred. The late John Cage, avant garde pianist and composer, attributes the origin of his "prepared piano" to Syvilla Fort, whom he met when she was a student at Cornish School of the Arts. Fellow Cornish student and New York choreographer, Merce Cunningham, once recalled that "she was very beautiful to watch." During the Depression of the 1930s Fort was choreographer for the Seattle Negro Federal Theatre Project. She became a member of Catherine Dunham's troupe in the late 1940s. After her retirement she taught dancing from her Park Avenue studio in New York, counting among her students singer Harry Belafonte, the late dance company founder, Alvin Ailey, and Hollywood movie actor Marlon Brando.

On January 24, 1992, B. F. Day School, *3921 Linden Avenue N.* acquired the Ghanian Ashanti name of Mate Misie, "I have kept what I have heard," in a traditional African naming ceremony. B. F. Day, Seattle's "oldest living school," is listed on the National Register of Historic Places and is one of several elementary schools in the county with a world culture curriculum centered around mathematics, geography, music and art. Day focuses on Africa. The students work with African artists in residence and correspond with pen pals from Africa. Sixty per cent of the students here are children of color, fourteen percent of African descent. In 1992 Day's staff authored a curriculum book, *We Are A World Family, Focus: Africa.* The school is headed by Carole Williams, who began her career in public education in 1970.

You may end this tour here, or proceed to the University District or Ballard.
To reach the University District, drive north on Fremont to 45th. Turn right onto 45th heading east to the University District.
To reach Ballard, take North 39th Street to Leary Way NW. Bear right to reach the commercial area and the Historic District.

Arts on the Avenue
Parking along University Way and neighboring streets is very limited. Buses frequently travel along the street and may be taken from Third Avenue downtown; others travel nearer the campus on 15th Avenue, one

block north of University Way. Several buses travel directly to the district from the eastside and the northend.

Along University Way are two African-run shops selling a variety of goods at reasonable prices. **Sahel International Arts and Crafts,** run by **Dior and Pappys Seck,** of the county's dozen or so Senegalese, is at *4541 University Way NE, 632-3272.* The store sells talking drums, tapes and records, in addition to art and jewelry. **Afrik Imports,** *4307-1/2 University Way NE, 632-4002,* has good quality batik and adinkra cloth, in addition to artwork and clothing at wholesale, as well as retail, prices. **La Tienda Folk Art Gallery,** *4138 University Way,* also carries African goods.

Three Ethiopian restaurants add distinctive flavor to the international cuisines found in this district. Memorable food is offered at: **The Wanza,** *6409 Roosevelt Way NE, 525-3950;* **The Nyala,** *5261 University Way NE, 524-8871,* which has reggae on Saturday nights; and the **Axum,** *4142 Brooklyn Avenue NE, 547-6848.*

Professor emeritus of Librarianship **Spencer Shaw** often appears in the Children's Book section of the University Bookstore, *4326 University Way NE, 634-3400,* for storytelling on Saturday afternoons. Professor Shaw has conducted institutes and workshops, and read and told stories around the country, and as far away as Australia. He narrated the films *Why the Sun and the Moon Live in the Sky,* and *Ashanti to Zulu.*

At the southwest corner of *41st and University Way* is the Glenn Hughes Playhouse, originally the Seattle Repertory Playhouse, founded by **Florence and Burton James,** University of Washington Drama Department faculty members. The Burtons, after featuring local African American actors in staging *In Abraham's Bosom* at the Repertory, were instrumental in spearheading the effort in 1936 to establish the **Seattle Negro Federal Theater,** a WPA project.

In its first year the federal theater had an acting company of seventy five, including singers and dancers. Most of its plays were presented here from 1936 to 1938. A few of the more popular or controversial ones were presented in downtown theaters, as well. In the last months of the project, a small theater at Rainier and Atlantic Street, no longer standing, was home to the group. Seattle actress **Sara Oliver Jackson** began her career at this theater in *Noah,* the first Negro Theater production.

Since its founding by the visionary Latino **Ruben Sierra,** and eleven actors of color in 1978, the Seattle Group Theatre at the University of Washington Ethnic Cultural Theatre, *3940 Brooklyn Avenue NE,* has been the principal venue for African American playwrights and actors since the closure of Black Arts West and the dormancy of the Paul Robeson Theatre at Langston Hughes. Former Black Arts West actor and artistic director, Tee Dennard, is often seen here, as is Ron Ben Jarrett. Seattle Community College drama teacher Tawnya Pettiford-Waites performed here in *Nappy Edges*, her poignant autobiographical choreopoem.

The Group's annual Multicultural Playwrights' Festival receives submissions from all over the United States. It moved to the Center House Theatre of the Seattle Center in January, 1993. Actor Tim Bond is theater director. The theater was designed by Benjamin McAdoo in 1969.

A year after McAdoo designed the Ethnic Cultural Theatre, he designed the second unit, the Ethnic Culture Center at *3931 Brooklyn Avenue NE* across the street from the theater, which houses offices and meeting space for several ethnic groups at the University. *Bearers of Culture*, an Eddie Walker mural, was painted for the Black Room in 1972. It is "dedicated to Afro-American women, unsung heroines of their people and humanity." Other large-scale Walker works may be viewed at the county courthouse,

*Sara Oliver Jackson
and Theodore Browne
in Noah,
the Seattle Negro
Federal Theatre's
first production, 1936.
(Courtesy of
Sara Jackson)*

the Douglass-Truth Library and the Carolyn Downs Clinic.

Beverly Mendheim at the center published *Ritchie Valens, First Latino Rocker* (Bilingual Review Press, ASU) the first biography of Ritchie Valens, in 1987. In 1990 she filmed a *famadihana,* or reburial ceremony, in the Malagasy highlands.

Sculptor James Washington, Jr. briefly studied painting at artist Mark Tobey's loft studio *near 42nd and University Way* until he was told by Tobey after a few sessions during the 1940s that, because of Washington's talent, he, Tobey, had nothing further to teach him.

The primary offering at Ezell's on the Avenue, *4216 University Way NE, 548-1455,* is fried chicken, but don't stop with just chicken. An assortment of deli offerings are as tasty as you will find anywhere. This restaurant is the branch of the original Ezell's on 23rd Avenue in the Central Area. The menus are the same at both places, and both offer catering and delivery.

The tour may end at this point, or you may make a quick detour to Ravenna to see the old Biggs family home before continuing with an exploration of some of the University of Washington campus.

Before her New York uncle sent her a two-seat Ford, **Lodi Biggs** walked from her family home at *1512 NE 70th Street* (∧) to the University of Washington where she earned her degree in pharmacy in 1917. She worked in laboratories and as a bacteriologist for the city health department prior to opening her "I-On-A-Co." **Crescent Biological Laboratory** which she operated in the Stimson Building on Fourth Avenue in downtown Seattle from the mid-1920s until the Great Depression. Lodi Biggs's nephew, **Howard Biggs,** concert pianist and organist, arranger, composer and director for the **Seattle Negro Federal Theater Project,** grew up in this house. He later arranged music for **Noble Sissle's** big band in New York.

From a Drummer's Perch to Hallowed Halls

A short tour of the University of Washington campus begins at the western entrance sidewalk, stair or footbridge near Campus Parkway. Drivers who enter the 41st Street entrance for parking will find wall signs indicating exits to the Henry Art Gallery.

The first building on this edge of the campus is the Henry Art Gallery, Seattle's first public art gallery, which opened in 1927. Its location was chosen to symbolize its accessibility to the city as well as the campus. In the 1930s the **Seattle Urban League** sponsored the **Harmon Award Exhibit** of **Negro Artists** here, the earliest gallery group showing of African American artists in King County. In the late 1960s the Henry featured the paintings of Denny Middle School teacher **Robert Colescott,** formerly of Seattle. *The Afro-American Tradition in Decorative Arts,* on exhibit touring under the auspices of the Links, a national African American women's organization, and sponsored by the local chapter, was featured here in 1979. *(LINKS c/o 12618 54th Avenue W., Mukilteo, WA 98275)*

Among the thesis shows held annually are those of African Americans completing their graduate studies in visual arts. The most recent was an exhibit of the work of sculptor **Russell Hamilton** in 1991. **Barbara Thomas,** who works for the City of Seattle as an arts administrator, and an established artist in her own right, presented her paintings here in a thesis show in 1977. One of her large paintings is part of the medical school's portable collection. Teacher preview nights are scheduled when exhibits

Interior of Zoe Dusanne's gallery at 1303 Lakeview Place, before it was razed for I-5 Highway construction. (Dearborn-Massar, Special Collections Division, University of Washington Libraries, negative no. 5354)

change, as are gallery tours, which are free if reserved ahead of time. Study guides to featured exhibits are also produced by the Henry.

The gallery holds a permanent collection of art works donated in memory of Zoe Dusanne, Seattle's first long-term private fine arts gallery owner. Dusanne began her own peerless collection during her stay in New York in the 1930s. At her gallery at *1303 Lakeview Place* which was razed for construction of the Interstate 5 (I-5) freeway, she championed many artists, American and foreign, who have since become internationally famous. The Seattle Art Museum held a *Tribute to Zoe Dusanne* exhibition of works by noted European and Northwest artists at the Modern Art Pavilion at Seattle Center in 1978. A memorial plaque in her honor was placed on the fifth floor *(#45, right hand side of corridor)*, at Children's Hospital, *41st NE and Sandpoint Way*, in the late 1970s.

Because of her light skin, she was often mistaken for white, and apparently did not assert her racial origin. She was the daughter of James and Letitia Denny Graves who came to Seattle from Council Bluffs, Iowa with their son, Giles, in 1906, and had offices in the old People's Savings Bank Building downtown at 204 Pike Street In 1915 Zoe, then known as Zola Mae Young, moved from Iowa with her young daughter, Theodosia, and joined her family at their Beacon Hill home. Shortly after her arrival, she rented rooms adjoining her parents' in the People's Building and operated an electrolysis studio until 1928 when she moved to New York.

Giles Graves also became a chiropodist and practiced for nearly fifty years in Seattle, most of the time in downtown offices. As a young man he was a strong swimmer. He recalled after his retirement, that while working at Fortuna Park (now Covenant Shores Retirement Community on Mercer Island), about 1911, he sometimes swam across Lake Washington to Leschi and, after resting, swam back again.

Jacob Lawrence, foremost American painter and retired faculty member, chose Meany Hall Performance Center, directly east of the undergraduate library, as the site for *Theatre* his enamel mural relating to the themes of tragedy and comedy and jazz. It was installed in 1985. Trained in Harlem, in a WPA program for artists in the 1930s, Lawrence came to Seattle as a visiting artist at the university in 1970. He returned to the city, with his wife, painter Gwendolyn Knight Lawrence, upon invitation in 1971 to join the university faculty. He is one of the most celebrated artists in America and his work is in various private and public collections in the United States and various countries around the world. Jacob Lawrence is the subject of two books: *Jacob Lawrence: American Painter* and *Jacob*

Lawrence: The Frederick Douglass and Harriet Tubman Series of 1938-40, both by Ellen Harkins Wheat (University of Washington Press.)

On the west edge of the campus is Imogen Cunningham Hall, the Women's Building during the Alaska Yukon Pacific Exposition. African American women from Tacoma had a booth here (**Colored Women's Exhibit**) and earned several awards for some of the handwork and art displayed. For two weeks during the 1909 A.Y.P.E., the Philippine Constabulary Band, which played for President Taft's inauguration, entertained fairgoers near the Geyser Basin, or frosh pond. The band was formed by Colonel **Walter Loving**, a young African American conservatory graduate who rounded up instruments in the Philippines and organized the band, which played for ceremonial occasions. A minstrel band also played at the fair.

In 1945 Pablo O'Higgins was commissioned by Seattle Local 541, Shipscalers, Drydock and Boatworkers Union to paint a fresco on concrete for their union hall, at 2221 Third Avenue. In 1955, the union sold their hall and moved to 23rd Avenue and East Madison Street, donating the mural to the university, which apparently forgot it. It was rediscovered by MECHA, a Latino student group in 1975, and moved to its present location, on the north wall of Kane Hall lobby, two years later.

The theme of racial harmony is depicted in the mural in words as well as representations of workers, for whom some of the union members were models. Membership in the shipscalers' union is overwhelmingly African American.

The **African-American Collection** in the Manuscripts and Archives Division of Suzzalo Library, consists of oral histories and memorabilia of African Americans in Washington, which were collected in the late 1960s. This valuable resource is open to students and independent researchers. The time period covered by the material extends from the mid-19th century to the lifetime of the persons interviewed.

Continue your tour of the campus by walking to Smith Hall, the southwest building on the Quad. Look up. Among the Dudley Pratt sculptured grotesques adorning the parapet of Smith Hall is one of an African drummer. It is at the east end of this 1939 building.

Miller Hall is the Southeast Quad building and southwest of the Music Building. The School of Education and the office of faculty member **Dr. James Banks**, specialist in multicultural education, are located here. Dr. Banks has conducted numerous workshops around the country and published several books on resources and techniques for teaching multi-ethnic curricula.

Master musicians, teachers and scholars from Africa have taught and studied at the School of Music, Ethnomusicology Division. They include Senegalese master sabar drummer **Abdoulaye Diop**, Mozambican

African drummer grotesque at Smith Hall by Dudley Pratt. (Bob Pickens, The People's Photo Studio, 1992.)

Solomon, master drummer **Yacub Addy** of Ghana, founder of **Ablade Bii,** and Zimbabweans **Ephat Mujuru,** and **A. Dumisani Maraire,** known locally as "**Dumi.**" Maraire is responsible for Seattle's national reputation as "Marimba Capital of the United States." In 1969 he formed the nation's first marimba ensemble in Seattle. In 1971 while at the university he made *The Mbira: The Music of the Shona People of Rhodesia,* (Nonesuch Records). Most marimba and mbira (thumb piano) players in the county are former Maraire students.

In the 1970s, saxophonist **Joe Brazil** taught jazz here, and made a controversial exit prior to founding a school of music at the **Central Area Motivation Program.**

The late **Dr. Elneta Cooper** taught her popular adult education classes to the "out of tune" here as well. Dr. Cooper, a founding member of the Canadian Music Research Council, began teaching at the university in 1972 and was an associate professor in the School of Music when she retired in 1992.

The Art Building is directly north of the Music Building. **Jacob Lawrence,** the first African American art faculty member, taught here from 1970 until his retirement in 1983. Between 1968 and 1991 artists **Florence Baker-Wood, Barbara Thomas** and **Russell Hamilton** studied here.

At the north end of the campus is Padelford Hall where **Charles Johnson** was teaching creative writing when his *Middle Passage* (Atheneum) won the National Book Award for fiction in 1990. Johnson came to the UW in 1976. He is a full professor in English, and has written a screenplay from the book. His other published novels are *Oxherding Tale* and *Faith and the Good Thing.* The Department of American Ethnic Studies headed by **Dr. Johnella Butler** is located in Padelford. Dr. Butler is a member of the county's Cultural Resources Division's management advisory group. **Professor John Walter** of the division is also in Padelford. He is the author of *The Harlem Fox,* and is collecting oral histories of African American athletes.

At the **Burke Museum,** *DB, 10, University of Washington, Seattle, WA 98195,* the Education Division, *206-543-5591,* has an African Art Classroom Display which may be borrowed for classroom use. This tour may be completed by visiting the Medical School to view **Barbara Thomas's** large acrylic painting which is periodically moved to different locations at the medical center. **Dr. Glover Barnes** conducted research and experimentation here for a male contraceptive. **Dr. Lois Price Spratlen** of the School of Nursing, is working with the **Mary Mahoney Nurses Club** to document the role of African American nurses in Seattle and other parts of the country.

Another way to end the tour is by traveling along Greek Row to *4637-21st NE,* where a former fraternity house was purchased by **Ray West** and his wife, **Marion,** in the early 1950s. The Wests provided housing for students of color at a time when it was all but impossible for persons of African descent to rent, or buy, in the district.

The property was in the name of Marion West, a Caucasian. Death threats were made against the couple, eggs were thrown, and a large cross was burned on the front lawn in 1958 to protest the Wests' presence. Mr. West, a civil rights' activist, was accused of Communist leanings and blacklisted. He later served as co-chair of the Mayor's Commission on Fair Housing. A different structure occupies the site today.

On to Sandpoint

To further explore this part of town depart the university from 45th Avenue NE and continue on to Sandpoint Way, (bus # 41 and #75) following the street past the entrance to Naval Base Puget Sound at 70th NE. Slow down to leave Sandpoint Way at the entrance to the National Oceanic and Atmospheric Administration (NOAA), 7600 Sand Point Way, two long blocks north. Enter the service road at the sign, turning left at the first parking lot entrance.

Walk north toward the water to view the large circular work of concrete and stone aggregate called *Knoll for NOAA.* This is the work of Chicago sculptor **Martin Puryear,** who the New York Times referred to as "a virtuoso with wood." He was born in Washington, D.C. in 1941, and studied at Yale. He has lived in Brooklyn, Sierra Leone, Sweden, and Japan. His work is influenced by West African woodworkers, Scandinavian furniture designers and Arctic carvers. This sculpture resulted from a Collaboration in Public Art involving five visual artists and the federal and city governments working with private citizens in 1983.

Puryear represented the United States at the Art Biennial held in Brazil in 1990. He was elected a member of the American Academy and Institute of Arts and Letters in 1992, a body whose membership is composed of one in a million Americans. *Five Artists at NOAA Casebook on Art in Public Places* (Fuller, 1985) describes the art and artists more fully.

Learn more about yourself or the area by exploring records at the National Archives and Records Administration, Pacific Northwest Region, *6125 Sandpoint Way, Seattle, WA 98115, 526-6500 or 526-6507. (Buses #74, #75, and #41 stop near the entrance).* Demand is heavy for this important genealogical and regional history research source. To avoid long waits for a microfilm reader and to reserve use, written requests should be made a month ahead.

In 1908, the **Dorcas Charity Club**, a group of African American women in Seattle, donated funds to purchase a bed, and to support what has become the Children's Hospital and Medical Center, *4800 Sand Point Way NE.* Since 1945 African American women have continued their contributions to Children's Hospital in the form of guilds. Two of the four organized among African American women are still in existence: the **Corinne Carter** and the **Idelle Vertner.** Carter founded the East Cherry YWCA, and Vertner was director of the branch for many years. This hospital is the parent of the **Odessa Brown Clinic** in the Central Area.

You may end this part of the tour by proceeding to Mountlake Boulevard, passing the stadium on the east. African American men helped to grade the playing field during the 1930s while working for the WPA.

Bear right to NE Pacific Street and enter Northlake Way to proceed to Ballard. Or you may proceed to Lake Washington Boulevard from Montlake Boulevard to begin a tour of Madison Street, or continue southward on Montlake to take a shorter tour of the area beyond Madison.

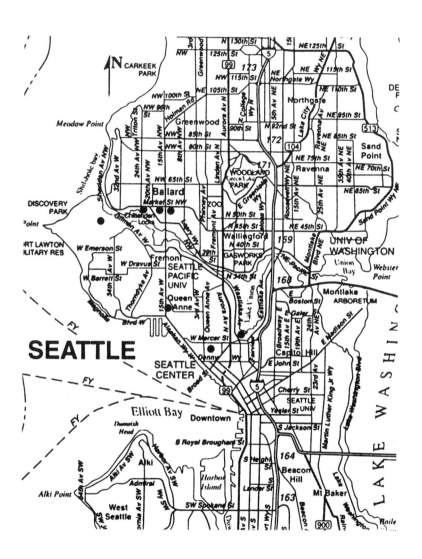

2.

Ballard, Magnolia, Queen Anne

Street Art, Sea Locks and Soundfests

William and Victoria Susandt and their daughter, Olive, are among the earliest African American residents recorded in Ballard. His barber shop was on the north side of Ballard Avenue between 20th and 22nd Avenue NW, in the town's commercial district during the 1890s. **Victoria Susandt** continued to live at their house on NW 56th Street between 22nd and 24th Avenue NW for many years after his death.

African American families have lived in various neighborhoods in Ballard from the turn of the century until the present. Until recent years their numbers were very small. The 1990 population of African Americans in Ballard was 837 or 1.6 percent of the total population of 39,322. This number represents a 126.8 percent increase over the 1980 total of 369.

Ballard Avenue is now in the heart of the Ballard Historic District. The sidewalks along the avenue bear reliefs by seven artists funded by Seattle's One Percent for Art program. **James Washington, Jr.'s** *Coelacanth,* in pink granite, is near the northeast corner of *5354 Ballard Avenue.*

After viewing this near-extinct fish, drive west on NW Market and follow the signs to see the real thing at the Ballard Locks of the Lake Washington Ship

Architect Horace Foxall at Lake Washington Ship Canal Administration Building, 1992. (James Carlson)

Canal. The Administration Building was designed in 1914 by the renowned Seattle architect, Carl Gould. In 1989, Horace Foxall designed the repair and restoration of some of the features of the building and the Cavanaugh House to their original design. Grandson of a carpenter and son of an artist, Foxall, the official Historic Preservation Architect with the Seattle District of the U.S. Corps of Engineers, developed the criteria for use in historic preservation by all the military branches in the United States. He received the Chief of Engineers Award of Merit for Military Programs in 1991, in recognition of his work in the repair and maintenance standards of historic buildings.

Architect Denice Hunt, as Planning and Development Specialist for the City of Seattle, developed a proposal to encourage and retain open space in the Lake Union/Ship Canal area. She received her Bachelor of Arts degree from Tufts University in 1969, and her Master of Architecture from Massachusetts Institute of Technology in 1976. Since her move to Seattle in 1977, Hunt has worked on projects ranging from historic restoration to managing and facilitating the review of projects by the Seattle Design Commission. Hunt has been with the city since 1984. She has received several awards, including fellowships and grants for study in Mali, Spain and Jamaica.

Having served as planning board member and guest editor of the *AR-CADE-Northwest Journal of Design*, she is the former editor of a column, the calendar, and an occasional contributor to the journal.

If you prefer continental African music or reggae, Ballard is a good place to hear it. The Ballard Firehouse, *at the corner of Market and Russell*, 784-3516, includes both forms among its featured offerings. The Backstage at Ballard, *2208 NW Market Street, 781-2805*, features live African music when musicians come through town.

Two periodicals may be helpful for advance planning. *Rhythmicentric of the Pacific Northwest*, is a monthly paper which reports the scheduling of African, Reggae, and Latin music events in the northern Pacific region. *Information: 206-282-0384 or write to 2810 15th Avenue W., Seattle, 98119. Rakumi Arts Newsletter*, an occasional publication with a local events calendar, provides information on the culture, as well as the music, of Africa. *For subscription and general information, write to Rakumi Arts International, 3809 Wallingford Avenue N., Seattle, WA 98103-8245.*

If you haven't spent too much time at the locks, and would like to continue exploring this part of town, leave Ballard by traveling southward along 15th Avenue W. Leave 15th W. at the Discovery Park exit, following West

Emerson Place until it ends at Gilman Avenue W. Continue along Gilman as it becomes Government Way, which leads to the park.

In 1889, Seaborn and Alzada Collins purchased two lots on Magnolia Boulevard which they sold to Allen Deans two years later. Whether or not either party built on the land is unknown, but at least one African American family has lived on Magnolia ever since their family home was erected in 1913. In 1990, slightly more than two percent, or 426, of Magnolia's 18,510 people were of African origin.

Fort Lawton and Discovery Park
A large part of Discovery Park is open for traveling by car, bicycle, or on foot, but some areas are posted and closed to the public. Bus #33 will take you there as well.

At the turn of the century, Magnolia Bluff landholders donated over seven hundred acres to the United States government for an army post. In 1972, the Army began the transfer of part of Fort Lawton to the city. Several years later it transferred another portion and the historic buildings around the parade ground to what is now Discovery Park. The first contingent of African American soldiers, the 25th Infantry Regiment, returned from the Philippines in 1909, and were stationed at Ft. Lawton. Most of these soldiers were veterans of the Spanish American War, many having seen battle in Cuba in 1898, and later in the Philippines, prior to their return to the United States. Until recent times some of the children of those soldiers lived in Seattle, and could recall living on the post. After a few years, African American troops were sent to other places.

Ft. Lawton was the second largest port of embarkation on the west coast during World War II. African American soldiers were once again stationed here, or passed through on their way to the Pacific theater of war. In 1944, a tragic chapter occurred in the city's history. African American soldiers, awaiting battlefield orders, became infuriated over their assignments to jobs that were far worse than those given to the Italian prisoners. They were restricted to a small segregated area of the base with few recreational opportunities while German and Italian prisoners-of-war were said to have been taken on tours and outings to various scenic areas of the state. In the ensuing uprising which followed one of the Italian POWs was lynched, resulting in the Army's largest court-martial of the war. Twenty-five soldiers were found guilty of rioting, and received sentences ranging from twelve to twenty-five years in prison. All received dishonorable discharges. The judge in this case was Leon Jaworski of Watergate fame.

You can easily spend the day hiking around the park, visiting the Daybreak Star Center of Native American Art, or joining in the nature walks, classes and programs offered by the park, 206-386-4236. Be sure to visit the Post Cemetery in the northeast section of the park, near the visitor's center. Several African Americans who fought in the Spanish American War are interred there, as are some of those who fought in World Wars I and II, the Korean and Vietnam Wars.

Leave the park and return to 15th Avenue W. via West Government Way.

Ribbin's Barbecue, *2201 15th Avenue W.*, *286-8055*, makes a convenient stop between Magnolia and Queen Anne Hill. Craig Jackson began this business with his brother, Gary, in 1984 when they bought a bankrupt Ballard restaurant and rebuilt it into a business which he operates mostly with young people generally thought unemployable. He has been in this location since 1991. A native of Kansas City, Jackson prides himself on alder smoked meat prepared in that city's famous style.

To reach Queen Anne Hill, continue along 15th Avenue W., which becomes Elliot, to Queen Anne Hill. Leave Elliot Avenue W. at West Mercer Street (West Mercer Place becomes West Mercer Street) to approach the Seattle Center. Bus riders will need to transfer to Buses #1, #2, or #13 from downtown.

Festivals and Art at Seattle Center
Some of the activities held each year at Seattle Center showcase performing, visual, and literary arts of people of African descent. The earliest of these is Festival Sundiata, the finest presentation of African and African American talent in the Northwest which is held at the Center House each February. Sundiata was a 12th Century Malian prince who left home to find his tribe's *griot*, the keeper of their history and culture, after he had been kidnapped by a neighboring tribe with whom they were feuding. The celebration expresses Sundiata's peoples' joy that the griot was found and returned safely.

This February festival has drawn an estimated thirty thousand people in the past. It features dancers and musicians from eastern, western, and southern Africa, as well as various parts of the United States. The work of local visual artists is exhibited here. A fashion show featuring local politicians and professionals, readings, book signings, writing workshops and a bookfair are also part of this festival, which is held during President's Day weekend. Music, from rap to reggae, and films on various topics from Africa, South America and the U.S. are offered. Admission to almost everything is free.

A few artists of African descent participate in the International Children's Festival which is held in May each year. Another opportunity to enjoy and observe African-derived art forms, some of them rarely heard or seen in the Northwest, is presented during Memorial Day weekend in May at the annual Northwest Folklife Festival held on the Center grounds. Famous and less-well known professional musicians from all over the

Lora Chiora Dye and members of her Sukutai Marimba Ensemble are frequent participants in Seattle Center festivals and programs. (Rex Rysted)

country play in concerts and presentations, and crafts are sold. Admission is free

Artists present their talents on the grounds and on stage in visual arts, literary arts and music, with activities for children during the Bumbershoot Festival held each Labor Day weekend. Ticket or gate admission entitles the bearer to attend all activities on a first-come, first-served basis.

In between these large annual events are several smaller ones occurring throughout the year, among them, special programs at the Children's Museum in the Center House on the fountain level. The Pacific Arts Center (PAC), 206-443-5437, which has a special African American History Month exhibit in February, has children's art on exhibit throughout the year and sponsors Artsreach, the PAC's outreach program that involves children throughout the city. KOMO TV sponsors an annual Kidsfair in August. The Seattle Center publishes a monthly events calendar which can be picked up at various locations in the Center House. *The customer service number is 206-684-7200.*

The papier mache sculpture near the entrance of the Pacific Arts Center building at the base of the stairway was made by ceramic and fabric artist **Monad**.

The Intiman Playhouse at the north end of the Seattle Center Grounds has two works by **James W. Washington, Jr.**: *Barbet*, a carved river boulder, completed in 1964 and funded by the Seattle Arts Commission, is in the entry court, and a smaller sculpture that is part of the Portable Works Collection which was funded by the Seattle Arts Commission and private donations. A badly weathered, untitled stone sculpture by Washington is part of the artwork designs by well-known local artists, which were completed in 1977, at the Betty Bowen Viewpoint at *Seventh Avenue W. and West Highland Drive.*

Of more monumental scope is the Queen Anne Pool, *1920 First Avenue W.,* which was designed by architect Benjamin McAdoo and Associates, and opened in 1977. McAdoo, and his associates, designed several public works projects in the county prior to his death in 1981.

Beginning with *Fences* in 1986, two of dramatist **August Wilson's** plays have been presented at the Bagley Wright Theatre prior to opening on Broadway in New York, with a third play presented in 1990. Wilson, winner of a Pulitzer Prize for *The Piano Lesson*, New York Drama Critics

Circle Awards and four Tony Award nominations, moved to Seattle from St. Paul in 1991.

Opening of the Jimi Hendrix museum at the former Seattle Art Museum's Modern Art Pavilion is planned for 1993.

As in other places in the county African Americans owned land on Queen Anne Hill and nearby. The largest parcel was purchased in 1866 by M.F. Monet whose seventeen acres on Lake Union were bordered by Dexter Avenue on the west, Westlake Avenue and Lake Union on the east, Highland Drive on the south and Galer Street on the north. Monet later sold this property, part of which presently belongs to the federal government and various private interests.

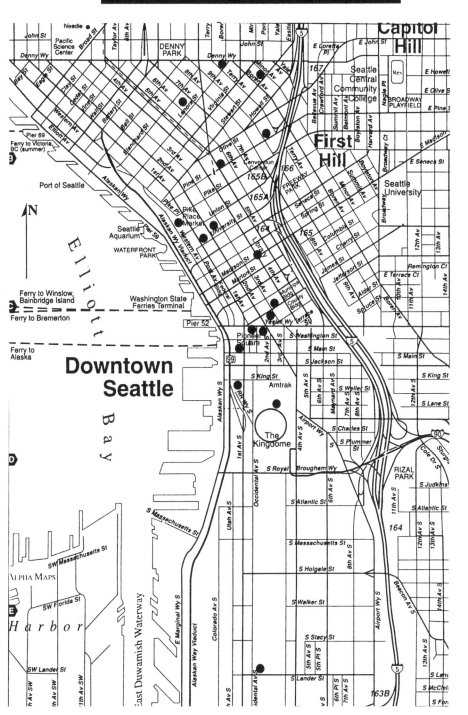

DOWNTOWN SEATTLE

Reprinted with the permission of the copyright owner, US WEST DIRECT, Publishers of the WHITE and YELLOW PAGES.

3.
Downtown Seattle

Pioneer Square Settlers and Successors

African American enterprise in King County began in the Pioneer Square area where residents operated small businesses in the earliest territorial days, mostly those providing services, such as barbershops, bathhouses, hotels and restaurants. Reflections of the activities of African Americans in downtown Seattle in the 19th century can be traced today. Most of Downtown may be traversed by foot. The Metro free-ride zone, which covers most of the Downtown, makes getting around easy and inexpensive.

African-born Manuel Lopes, the city's first African American settler and its first barber, arrived on a sailing ship in 1852. After settling here he sent back to Boston for Seattle's first barber chair, which was brought around the Horn to the village of muddy streets, tree stumps and a few houses in the 1850s. His little white house and barber shop stood mid-block on First Avenue, just south of the pergola. (Published accounts fail to establish whether it stood on the east or the west side of the street.)

In 1869 William Hedges sold a quarter of the lot at the northwest corner of Occidental Park to ship's cook John Closson for five hundred dollars. Closson was later convicted and confined to the territorial prison at Steilacoom for selling bootleg liquor from the log cabin he built there. At the turn of the century Lloyd and Emma Ray operated the Olive Branch Mission near Pioneer Square, where they ministered to poor, discouraged miners returning from the Klondike.

Denice Hunt, architect, and the city's Urban Designer, was responsible for the development of the Pioneer Square Historic District guidelines, and authored the revision of the Pioneer Square Plan. She was also responsible for the development of the design concepts and guidelines for the Downtown harbor-front, including the integration of public art projects there.

Seattle's waterfront is almost as accessible today as it was in the city's early years. Some of the 19th century African American businesses were on wharfs or near the waterfront, as are some today. Emmatrice Limited, African Imports, at *71 Yesler Way, Seattle, WA 98104, 624-9154*, features a wide variety of decorative art, jewelry, furniture and clothing. Much of the clothing is made from fabric dyed in age-old West African traditional patterns. The shop's Ghanian owners, will ship orders upon request.

In the early 1980s, artists Roy Sahali, Anthony Washington, and Richard Sarto operated the cooperative Picaro Press Studio Gallery 75, *75 Yesler*. In 1985, Sahali opened the Edge Gallery at *81 South Washington Street* to bring to the public artwork that escaped the notice of the main galleries in town. Sahali, a painter who curated Festival Sundiata's visual arts exhibition for several years, is now coordinator of the Southern Africa desk at the American Friends Service Committee. Sarto lives and works as an artist in the California Bay Area.

Starms Washington, a former governmental technical writer and journalist, began Picaro Press/Scriptorium 300, *300 South Washington Street, 624-3036*, at 71 Yesler, in 1977. He specializes in limited edition letterpress books, broadsides, reproductions, prints and cards. Washington is also press agent for reggae, African and salsa bands, and business agent for visual artists. *Open by appointment.*

The Bread of Life Mission, at *97 South Main Street*, is where Ron Hayes, a former alcoholic, began work as a kitchen helper. By the late 1960s Hayes

William Hedges sold the northwest corner of Occidental Park to John Closson in 1869.
(Don Mumford)

was head of this mission, which ministers to homeless and transient men. He later became Food Minister for the Union Gospel Mission. Now retired and living in Renton, part of his life story has been depicted in comic book form and will be published by the Peace Garden Mission in Chicago. Aired in the county on KDWN, a Christian broadcasting station, are parts of *Unshackled,* the autobiography of the Rev. Hayes, an ordained minister.

Very few of the territorial businesses in the area survived into statehood, but African Americans continued to locate there. Shortly after **Irene Patterson Woodson** arrived in Seattle in 1897 with her husband, **Zacharias**, she opened a cigar store at what is now the west end of the public parking lot between Yesler and James, First and Second Avenues, which is sometimes referred to as the "sinking ship." Her son Fred recalled in 1976: "She opened before any other cigar store and she transacted enough business to close the shop by the time the next cigar store had opened. At that time the business was all walk-in trade and the Pioneer Square area was the center of all activities." Zacharias Woodson hired African American men to help him operate shoeshine stands in Pioneer Square. A few years after 1900, this hardworking, frugal couple became owners of several rooming houses, including one at *1412 Fourth Avenue*, on the site of Clyed's Cameras, another at the rear of *1216 Second Avenue*, which is occupied by part of the Washington Mutual Tower, and a third at *1530 Fifth Avenue* at the corner of Fifth and Pine where Jay Jacobs stands.

The **New Orleans Creole Cafe,** *114 First Avenue South, 622-2563,* is one of the most popular night spots in Seattle, featuring live jazz, blues or zydeco every night. Some of Seattle's most accomplished jazz performers play here. One such performer is percussionist **Clarence Acox,** who has recorded two albums and directs the award-winning Garfield High School jazz band. He and trumpet and fluegelhorn player **Floyd Standifer** may be heard here

Denice Johnson Hunt, City of Seattle's Urban Designer.

on a regular basis. Others who grew up in the Seattle jazz scene occasionally play here when they return to town.

Jazz devotees should be aware of two highly reliable sources on jazz, in addition to the weekly newspaper entertainment sections. *Earshot Jazz*, a monthly magazine, features articles on jazz and announcements on future events. Free copies may be picked up at Seattle Public Library, record stores, jazz clubs, and several places in the University District. *Subscriptions are available from Earshot Jazz, 3429 Fremont Place, #303, Seattle, WA 98103, (206) 547-6763. Riff / The Magazine of the Washington Jazz Society* is a monthly calendar of jazz events which is available at many of the same places as Earshot Jazz. *Write to WJS, P.O. Box 2813, Seattle, WA 98111. For information call Ed Foulks, 324-2794.*

Ghanaian woodcarver, **Atta Newman Adjiri**, opened the **Adjiri Arts Gallery** in the Grand Central Arcade, *214 First Avenue South, 464-4089*, in 1991. Blending old techniques with new, this artist devotes his gallery almost exclusively to the African mask.

Rental space was difficult to obtain, but African American professionals have had offices in the Interurban Building (also known as the Pacific Building) from the beginning of the century. **Ed Hawkins** and **Andrew Black** had their law offices there from 1901 until their deaths in 1912 and 1918. Bail bondsman **Prentice Frazier** had his first office there before moving to Third Avenue.

In this building is **Cheryl Glass Designs**, *102 Occidental South, (206) 467-7000*, which is diagonally across from Irene Woodson's old cigar store. You won't see designs like these anywhere else. The business is owned and operated by **Cheryl Glass**, one of the country's few female race car drivers, and the only professional African American woman racing driver in the United States. She is president, driver and co-owner (with her father **Marvin Glass**) of the Glass Racing Team. Her first business "**Cheryl's Ceramics**," a wholesale operation which included Marshall Field among her clients, was begun at age nine, the year she began amateur racing. Glass was a gifted student who graduated high school at sixteen, before attending Seattle University for three years where she, like her mother and father, studied engineering. She was a photographer's model and was selected a Seafair Princess in the late 1970s. The gown she created for her 1983 wedding, a dress adorned with thousands of pearls, sequins and crystals brought numerous requests for her services, which resulted in her opening this custom-design wedding dress and special events service.

This place of elegance provides full service for weddings and special occasions. Original designs are made to specifications using the finest fabrics, beadwork and antique laces. The house also offers catering services, and custom printing. Cheryl Glass was recognized as the "Most Outstanding

Young Designer" in a "Salute to Pacific Northwest Black Designers" in the 1980s. She was honored in 1989 by the National Coalition of 100 Black Women. Her work has been featured nationally in fashion and style coverage. Her fashion drawings are on display at the design studio, as are some of her executions. Cheryl Glass' sister, **Cherry**, a trained commercial airlines pilot, graduated from Seattle Pacific University at age nineteen.

In 1988 **Terry D. Morgan** and **Roy L. Monceaux** opened an art gallery at the southwestern corner of the ground floor of the Smith Tower at *502 Second Avenue*. In the course of its brief existence they brought to Seattle such innovations as the use of video to attract passersby. The first exhibit of hip hop graffiti art in Seattle was shown here, as were the mid-19th century paintings and engravings of lithographer, **Grafton Tyler Brown.** His painting of Mount Rainier in the early 1880s, now in the Washington State Historical Society collection in Tacoma, is the earliest identified artistic creation of an African American in the state.

Morgan, local impresario and musician, was the first producer of Festival **Sundiata.** Monceaux, former gallery partner in Los Angeles and San Francisco, and now of New York, is an artist, lecturer and curator.

Art at the Market

Few visitors to Seattle fail to visit the **Pike Place Market.** Most African American vegetable peddlers worked in the southern and eastern areas of the county rather than in the market. Cayton's *Weekly* newspaper mentions

Designer Cheryl Glass fits a customer at her fashion studio. (CNN Photo)

an African American vegetable vendor couple in 1918, but artists are the only regular vendors today.

One of the fixtures among artists is **John Jenkins,** maker of chrome, copper and stainless steel jewelry who often sees repeat customers from many places in the country at his day stall. A different style is seen at the stall of **Linda Marie Designs** which features hand-painted tee shirts and other clothing.

Njambi Gishuru of Kenya began selling East African art at street fairs in 1984. She opened **African Imports,** *1530 Post Alley, #6, 624-6092,* in 1986, and expanded into a second shop at Pier 57's Bay Pavilion in 1992. The year before Gishuru published *Authentic African Cooking,* a book of Kikuyu and other East African recipes, which is available at the stores.

The **African Women's Association** is associated with women's groups in the United States and abroad. It was formed in 1992 to encourage women from different countries to work together to learn about each other's cultures, and to acquaint the public with African cultures through public events. They meet the first Friday of each month at the American Friends Service Committee building, *814 NE 40th, 632-0500.* For more information write Ufilia Davis, president, P.O. Box 22063, Seattle, WA 98122-0063.

Young break dancers disappeared from downtown streets with the decline in popularity of that dance, but street corner musicians can sometimes be seen in various locations, as can street corner artists. At the Pike Place market, one may occasionally see a gospel quartet, or more frequently, **Dukadu,** a poet who came of age in the 1960s and plays both saxophone and bass violin. Former boxer and painter **Danny Mayes,** who once sold his watercolor renderings of Seattle exclusively from the sidewalk, is now featured in galleries around town and may be seen vending from the sidewalks as well. **Glenn Clanton,** often seen at Third and Pine, began crafting stained glass as part of therapy from an injury he sustained in 1986. His small-scale work sometimes includes old glass from larger pieces.

Praises and Pleasures

The only African American church downtown is the **Bright and Morning Star Baptist Church** (Rev. Derrick Boseman, pastor) at the corner of *1900 Boren Avenue at Stewart Street.* The **Total Experience Choir,** the noted gospel singing group, which has appeared all over the state and sung in several cities in the nation and abroad, is based here. *For information, call 322-7904.* Choir founder and director, **Patrinell Wright** received the 1991 Washington State Heritage Award for her contribution to the enrichment of the state's heritage. The church sponsors a night shelter for homeless men.

African derived dance and costume of Brazil are the most recent and exciting strains joining the increasingly varied cultural offerings of peoples of African extraction. It was introduced to the public in the debut of Alujah, led by its founder, Elisio Pitta, at the Washington performance Hall in 1991. The troupe's rehearsals may be visited at their Aluja Center for Cultural Development, at 2017 Terry Street, 623-7483, on Monday and Wednesday evenings.

A few blocks away on the east side of *Ninth Avenue, between Olive Way and Pine Street,* are four concrete and granite planters at Convention Place Metro Station which are the work of New York artist Maren Hassinger (1990), who suggested the plantings. Her Norway maple *(acer platanoides)* tree relief designs on iron tree grates may be seen at the "Tree Grate Museum" on the Convention Place sidewalk. To get the full effect of the grates and look at the base of the trees, walk along Third Avenue between Union and Pine Streets.

Since the 1970s Dimitrou's Jazz Alley, *Sixth and Lenora, 441-9729* has featured such big-name jazz artists as Lionel Hampton, Dizzy Gillespie, Hugh Masakela and Seattle's own Earnestine Anderson as well as other of the county's superb local jazz artists. The fabulous Anderson moved from Houston to Seattle with her family in 1944. She is featured in the *I Dream a World* book (Stewart, Tabori and Chang) and traveling exhibition, and is one of several famous jazz artists depicted in oil portraits at Jazz Alley. The portraits are painted by Dean Williams who came to Seattle from Washington, D.C. in 1985. His *Simpatico,* a collection of studies of nudes was exhibited in a restaurant at the Wallingford Center in 1991. Working mostly in oils, Williams recently taught at the School of Visual Concepts, and numbers among his several commissions the official 1990 Goodwill Games poster.

Included in the Sheraton Hotel and Towers collection, *(1400 Sixth Avenue at Pike Street)* of more than two thousand artworks is James Washington, Jr.'s *Obelisk with Phoenix and Esoteric Symbols of Nature.* Sculpted in 1982 of carnelian granite, it is near the west wall on the main floor. Inside Fuller's Restaurant on the first floor near the west pillar is Jacob Lawrence's design for the poster for the Bellevue Arts and Crafts Fair, a gouache on paper which was painted in 1981. The hotel's collection guide is available on request.

In 1968, James Washington, Jr. was commissioned by the Seattle Public Library, using privately donated funds, to sculpt a work in memory of Eugenia Raymond, a former head of the Art and Music Department of the Seattle Public Library. His *Kinship of All Life,* bird, animal and fish designs with various symbols, is carved in relief on a slab of Egyptian pink granite. Washington's four sculptured, relief-carved benches of black granite at the Sea-First Building, directly across the street from the library on Fourth Avenue, were sculpted in 1968-69. Part of his *Series in Creation*, they reflect the artist's deep religious conviction. His *Renewness of Life*, a granite sculpture may be viewed at the YWCA, *Fifth Avenue and Seneca Street*. Donald King and Associates provided planning and design for the library's writer's room addition which will be converted from an unused foyer and adjacent outdoor area. The Capital Projects Department at the library is managed by architect Dwight Rives.

One of the lighter notes in Downtown art is at Westlake Park. The Children's Art Project, at Westlake and Pine, is the result of Denice Hunt persuading city officials to install the artwork. When walking through the park, be sure to look down to see the bronze tiles set in a basket-weave pattern scattered around the park bearing the artwork and games of the city's children. Hunt was also responsible for the inclusion of such public art as the water wall fountain and the large sculptural pieces at the park.

African Americans lived downtown from the city's beginning. When Charles and Eva Ellis Harvey came to Seattle from Minnesota in 1886 they swept out the loft of a barn in Belltown where they lived until they could find better accommodations. Shortly afterwards, they moved to a small house on Second Avenue at the site of the new Seattle Art Museum, from which Charles Harvey and James Booker operated the Handicap Company, a painting and carpentry business. It was at this site that Eva Harvey held her infant daughter, Gertrude, in her arms and watched the beginning of the conflagration in 1889 that eventually destroyed the town. Among the African American businesses lost in the fire were a boot and shoemaking shop, a restaurant, an employment agency, a real estate firm, a hotel, and two barbershops. Several owners did as other business people did: cleared away the rubble, hung out a shingle and, in a few days, resumed business as usual, in a tent.

In the late 1890s Harvey, then a full-fledged contractor, had an office in the basement of the Pioneer Building in Pioneer Square. The house that Booker built in East Madison after the turn of the century is still standing.

The Katherine White Collection of African Art is the basis of one of the more noted exhibits at the Seattle Art Museum, *100 University Street*. Textiles, ceremonial masks, utilitarian objects, and jewelry drawn from sixty-seven different African cultures are featured in three galleries on the third floor. Continuous videos depicting the use of the objects may be viewed in the galleries. The museum also has works of local artists, James Washington Jr. and Jacob Lawrence. *Jacob Lawrence, American Painter*, a retrospective of the work of the artist, drew the largest crowd

Jacob Lawrence
poster.
(Seattle Art Museum
Collection)

ever attending an exhibition opening at the museum's Capitol Hill building in 1986. Former Seattle resident **Robert Colescott's** paintings were featured in a 1989 retrospective at the museum. Some special exhibits have been built around items in the African Art Collection, as well as touring exhibitions from other museums and galleries.

The **African, African-American, and Caribbean Arts Council** is one of seven sponsored by the museum. Open to Seattle Art Museum members, the council offers opportunities to explore African-derived cultures in depth through lectures, tours, workshops and seminars. *Information: Council Office, 654-3136.*

The museum has an **African Treasure Box** which may be borrowed for classroom use. *Call the Services for Schools Program at the museum, or write to: Services for Schools, Education Department, Seattle Art Museum, P.O. Box 22000, Seattle, WA 98122-9700.*

Diagonally across the street from the museum is **Streeter/Dermanis Architects,** *185 University,* a mid-sized firm which was begun in 1967 by **Mel Streeter,** a University of Oregon graduate from Pasadena, California. The firm has designed and constructed buildings around Puget Sound, for which several have received awards for design excellence. Streeter has been active in the **Architects in the Schools** program.

Most of the young African American architects in the county have gained experience working at this firm. A more seasoned architect, **Sam Cameron,** came to the firm in 1989 after working at McKinley Architects where, prior to his leaving, he was part of the design team for the **Washington Mutual**

Tower, *1201 Third Avenue,* and the First Interstate Center *at 999 Third Avenue.*

The office at *609 Third Avenue* was formerly that of bail bondsman **Prentice I. Frazier.** A biographical sketch of Frazier, possibly written by his nephew, **Otis Bean,** states that in this business Frazier, "either became a friend or an adversary of most of the policemen, prosecutors, and judges, and their staffs, in their criminal justice endeavors."

Near the top of the elevators on the north side of the first floor of the King County Courthouse, *516 Third Avenue,* is a plaque which commemorates the renaming of King County in honor of the **Rev. Dr. Martin Luther King, Jr.** instead of its original namesake, William Rufus Devane King, a slaveholder who was vice-president of the United States in 1853 for a short time before his death.

The plaque was placed in the Court House in 1989. The redesignation was approved by County Council vote in 1986 following the bill's introduction by county councilmen **Ron Sims,** African American, and representative of the Fifth District representing most of the area south of the Lake Washington Ship Canal and north of Renton, and **Bruce Laing** of the sixth district representing about one-third of the east side of Lake Washington. King County's first African American woman judge, **Norma Johnson Huggins,** presides from chambers in this building. She is one of four African American judges on the Superior Court. The most senior member of

Martin Luther King, Jr. Commemorative plaque at the King County Courthouse.
(Debra Brockway)

the group, **Charles V. Johnson,** has served since 1981. **Justice Charles Z. Smith,** the first African American judge in King County, has served on the Washington State Supreme Court since 1988.

By now you've probably glimpsed at least part of the domed stadium. In addition to watching African American professional athletes, the small Royal Brougham Sports Museum at the Kingdome has related exhibits which may be viewed when there are no daytime events. Jacob Lawrence's huge *Games,* his first enamel on steel mural, was installed at the dome in 1979. Funded by the county's One Percent for Art Program, it hangs near the second level bridge ramp.

The stadium is easily reached from Downtown via Second Avenue S. by crossing Washington at an angle, and avoiding the Second Avenue S. extension. From I-5 take the Spokane Street exit (163) to Fourth Avenue South, heading north to Royal Brougham Way. Turn left, and follow the signs. Buses #7, #14, and #36 may be taken from Third Avenue downtown to Jackson Street, the closest stop to the stadium.

Franglor's Cajun and Creole Cafe, *547 First Avenue South, 682-1578,* a few blocks south of the stadium, features New Orleans cuisine in hefty servings of notable food, which, should you have the room, may be topped off with pecan or sweet potato pie. The memorabilia on the walls is almost as interesting as the menu.

Most of the early land purchases by African Americans were in, or near, Downtown. In 1869 **George P. Riley** purchased twelve acres on Beacon Hill for the Oregon-based **Workingmen's Joint Stock Association.** In 1870 he purchased an additional fifteen acres for the group of small business men and women in the vicinity of South Lander Street and First Avenue South. It was under water at the time of the purchase, but over the years the area was filled with earth removed from Beacon Hill and other high places in Seattle.

One hundred and twenty years later, an African American entrepreneur, **Cyril Miller,** and his wife, Renee, moved to the area to continue their gourmet smoked poultry business, **Seattle Super Smoke,** *2454 Occidental S. at South Lander, (206) 625-1339.* Begun in the Ravenna area in 1983 by Miller, a former sky cap superintendent, whose wife, Renee, serves as accountant, the business produces moist, flavorful smoked chicken, turkey and other meats, as well as salmon which is served in over two hundred Washington restaurants, and in first class cabins on airplanes. Much of their business is wholesale, but retail customers may purchase items to carry home, or stop in for lunch. Tables are available for eating outside on sunny days, as well.

In a thank-you letter to Cyril Miller in 1989 Master Chef Julia Child wrote: "Thank you so much for the great selection of smoked poultry. I really think it's the best I've ever had because it's so juicy and tastes of what it is." Child was so enthused that she peddled some of the poultry to California restaurants to encourage them to order more from the Millers.

WEST SEATTLE, SOUTH PARK, VASHON

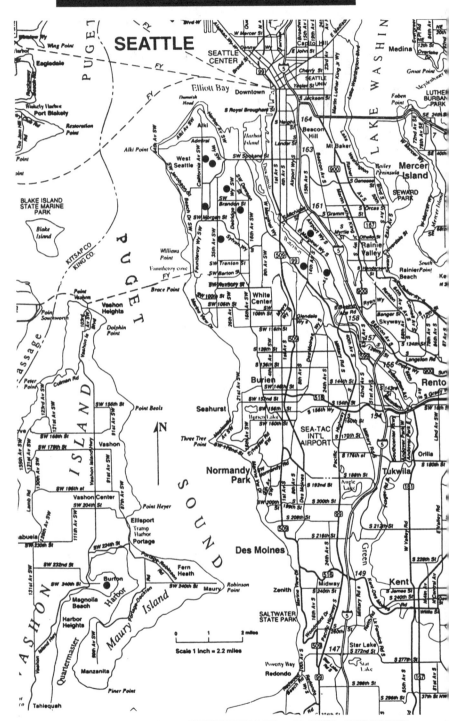

Scale 1 Inch = 2.2 miles

4.

West Seattle, South Park, Vashon

Westerly to Land's End

All traces of the chicken farm operated by Dan Myers and his wife, Clara, at the turn of the century were obliterated in the expansion of the Boeing Company. During the Nome gold rush, Myers thought he could do better in the goldfields, but soon found out that, "Nome is not what it is cracked up to be," as he described his adventure to a Seattle *Republican* reporter upon his return. He resumed work at his chicken ranch, which he and his wife operated up to World War I.

While evidence of the Myers farm has been paved over, the largest structure associated in any way with an African American in King County stands at *9010 East Marginal Way S.* on the perimeter of Boeing Field. Consisting of eighty-four thousand square feet, it formerly housed the Federal Aviation Administration headquarters. This building, which won an award for design excellence upon its completion in 1972, is a fine example of the work of the Streeter/Dermanis architectural firm. It is now called the 777 Group Building.

A few sources mention the presence of anonymous African Americans in the South Park area in the 19th century. The Bailey brothers operated a barber shop in the commercial area for several years after the turn of the century. The 238 African Americans living there in 1990 represent a 400 percent increase over the 47 who were there in 1980. The work of architect Donald King is readily visible in the area. King earned his Master of Architecture degree in 1978 from the University of California, Los Angeles, with a concentration in health care facility design which has been used in the continuing expansion of the Sea-Mar Community Health Center, *8720-8800 14th Avenue S.* Since 1986 King has developed plans for the expansion of the dental clinic, the family health residence wing, a child development center and a skilled nursing center.

The first Northwest Marimba Festival was held at the South Park Community Center, *8319 Eighth Avenue S.*, in 1991. It was coordinated by Sheree Sparks, founder of Anzanga Marimba and Dance, *684-4757.*

West Seattle

African Americans living in West Seattle are thought by many people to have first moved there as residents of the High Point Housing Project. Land ownership, however, dates to the 1890s. **Allen Deans,** who purchased property in many parts of the county, bought two lots on the 3700 block of 40th Avenue SW, and two on the 3900 block of West Charleston across the street from the city water standpipe in 1890. Shortly afterwards, veterinarian **Samuel Burdett** and his wife moved to their home in West Seattle and lived there from the 1890s until they moved to Benton County to take up homesteading in 1905. Sawmill and steel mill workers also purchased small homes in the 1920s in order to be near their work. Like other Seattleites in the years before World War I, young African Americans visited Alki on some of their outings.

After much difficulty with discriminatory practices by city golf clubs, **Madeline Wright** was accepted by West Seattle Women's Club in 1958. The Jackson Park Women's Golf Club also accepted an African American member that year. The admission of men who were known to be of African descent did not take place until the 1960s. Wright and her husband fought diligently for the integration of clubs supported by public money which had racially-exclusive policies.

West Seattle is the home of sculptor **Weldon Butler,** whose work was featured in an exhibition at the West Seattle Cultural Gallery in 1992 .The work of the **Streeter-Dermanis** firm may be seen at the gymnasium of the High Point Housing Project.

The 1,846 African Americans in the area from Fauntleroy to Highland Park in 1980 increased 80% in ten years, numbering 3,337 or 7% of the

Boeing Company occupying land in 1957 once owned by Dan Myers chicken farm.
(King County Regional Archives)

total population of 29,621 in 1990. In the Alki-Admiral district the population rose to 2% of the total population, increasing 164% from 247 to 653 during the same period. Small African American businesses—a grocery store, a restaurant—and the **Full Gospel Pentecostal Federated Church,** *5071 Delridge Way. SW, 935-1511,* have followed the population growth.

Vashon Island
Forty-two African Americans live on Vashon Island. A logging contractor on Vashon, who went bankrupt in the 1850s, bears the same name as an African American man who later moved to Olympia and entered the barber's trade. Whether this was the same person in both places has not been determined with any certainty.

George Washington, one of the state's African American town founders, platted Centralia in 1873. He had one son, George, Jr., who died in 1912 from pneumonia contracted as a result of injuries sustained in fighting the fire that destroyed the main building of Vashon College on the hill northwest of Burton.

A 150 page unpublished history of Seattle publisher **Horace R. Cayton** was written by Dr. Tom Douglas and donated to the Vashon-Maury Island Heritage Society in 1991.

TUKWILA TO FEDERAL WAY

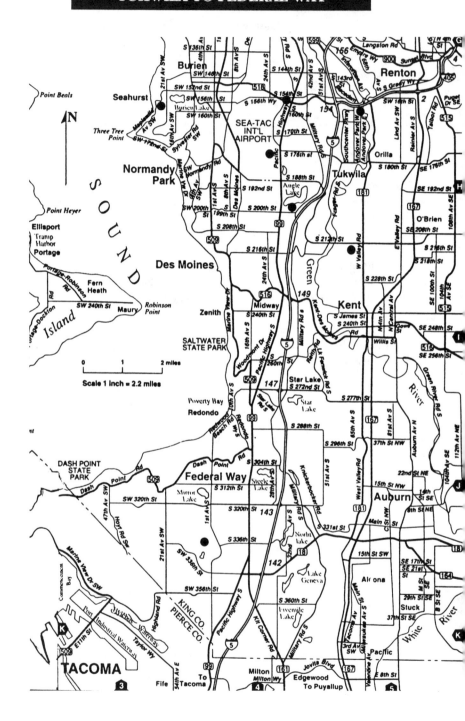

5.
Tukwila to Federal Way

Public Works and Prayers, Too

With the increase in jobs in the suburban areas in the 1980s, and the tremendous increase in city housing costs, about one-third of the county's African American population now resides outside of Seattle. In the 1980s about seventy-five percent of the county's increase in the African American population was outside of the city.

Several of the public buildings in this part of the county were designed and constructed by African American architects and their firms. Here, as in Seattle, African Americans are engaged in public service and businesses, and are beginning to establish churches, the first signs of organized life.

An outing to look at the places mentioned here takes about half a day from Seattle or Bellevue, or twice as long should you decide to go inside the buildings, attend a church service, have a swim and a picnic, view the art, or slow your pace and think about some of the folk who lived here in the past, and the life that newer residents are making for themselves today.

Tukwila

A few African Americans were reported as residents of the Tukwila area shortly after the turn of the century, but most are of more recent origin. The 1990 census reports seventeen percent of the city's population of 11, 874 as people of color, including 755 African Americans. In 1968, **Benjamin McAdoo** and his associate, **Richard Hull**, designed the King County Blood Center's Southcenter Branch, *130 Andover Park E.*, and designed additions to the building some years later. McAdoo designed the house at *2648 SW 167th Place* which was chosen "Home of the Month" for 1956 by the Washington State Chapter of the American Institute of Architects.

Sea-Tac

The new city of Sea-Tac had 1,029 African American residents in 1990. They have made notable contributions have been made to the city's development. *The Sea-Tac Community Newspaper*, the city's first, is published by Renton resident **Gloria McCoy Waller**. This monthly is an outgrowth of the publisher's bimonthly *Ethnic-American Experience magazine* which began in 1991. The newspaper includes news of Sea-Tac and neighboring communities in the southern end of the county. McCoy began her journalistic experience in New York and worked as a writer for the *FACTS* newspaper in Seattle.

The **Riverton Heights Post Office,** *15250 32nd Avenue S.,* was designed by **Benjamin McAdoo** and his associates, in 1974. Architect **Sam Cameron,** an associate of the **Streeter/Dermanis** firm, was in charge of the management of the architectural design of the new Sea-Tac expansion parking terminal which opened in 1992.

Kent

William A. Scott and his wife, **Pauline,** who moved to Kent following the destruction of his barber shop in the Seattle fire of 1889 are the earliest known residents of African descent in Kent. On their land they operated a successful truck farm, selling to commission houses in Seattle. The Scotts also sold timber and leased roadway to lumbering companies to cross their land between Second Street and State Avenue now in downtown Kent.

From a solitary couple one hundred years ago, the African American population grew to 1,455 in 1990. Their household income is slightly higher here than the average White household income.

By 1890, Seattle's African American population was familiar with Kent. The M. K. Kelly's baseball team traveled here to play the local team that year, or on occasion, a team from Tacoma. The first "Juneteenth" celebra-

King County Central Blood Bank and Office Building was designed by Benjamin McAdoo, King County's first successful African American architect, and his associate, Richard Hull. (Photographic Illustrators)

tion held in the county was celebrated in Kent by the African American communities of Tacoma and Seattle in 1890. This holiday marks the effective date of the edict issued by the military governor of East Texas declaring that from June 19, 1865, all workers must be paid for their labor. This was a strengthening of the Emancipation Proclamation which did not free the slaves in areas under the occupation of federal troops, and in other areas where the proclamation was ignored.

Kent has one African American church, **Center of Faith Church of God in Christ**, *25628 101st Avenue SE, 630-3367* which was founded in 1989 under the leadership of its present pastor, the **Rev. Wilbur Vincent**. The membership of about 125 adults, and an almost equal number of children, is composed of members of the military, and workers at Boeing, in banks, corporations and stores. Their outreach includes a prison ministry, "Helping Hand" ministry for emergencies, and a street ministry in Kent and Seattle.

Works of art by African American artists **Phillip Lewis** and **Barbara Thomas** which were funded by the Washington State Arts Commission are in the **Portable Collection** of the **Kent School District**. The **Jube Gallery** and frame shop on First Avenue S. represents painter **Eric Salisbury**, a Kent resident. As an associate of the McKinley Architects firm **Sam Cameron** was project manager for the design of **Van Doren's** office park on the West Valley Highway south of 212th Street in Kent.

Des Moines
The **Angle Lake Park Dressing Rooms**, *19048 Pacific Highway S.*, is one of the early public works projects designed by **Benjamin McAdoo** and associates and another tangible reminder of African Americans' contribution to the development of the county. The African American population in Des Moines in 1990 was 648.

Auburn
The **Auburn City Hall**, *25 West Main*, in downtown Auburn was designed and constructed by the **Streeter/Dermanis** architectural firm in 1979. The fifty thousand foot structure includes offices for the mayor, city council members, the City Council chamber, a cafeteria, police department and detention facilities, as well as other departments. Mel Streeter began the firm in 1967.

A University of Oregon School of Architecture graduate, **Mel A. Streeter** was born in Pasadena, California, and influenced in his career choice by his fellow Californian, the late **Benjamin McAdoo**, Seattle's first successful

Pacific Chief of Police, Al Lee, is the first and only African American to serve in that capacity in the state.

The Auburn City Hall was designed and constructed by the Streeter/Dermanis architectural firm in 1979. Mel Streeter began the firm in 1967. (Don Mumford)

African American architect. The **Boeing Fire Station** at the Auburn plant was designed by McAdoo and his associates in 1979.

Through the years a small number of African Americans, including a few railroad workers in the late 1910s and 1920s, have lived in and around Auburn. The 1990 census lists 452, among them sculptor **Marita Dingus,** who was born there, and more recently, rap star **Anthony Ray,** better known as **Sir Mix-A-Lot,** who, after two successful albums in the late 1980s, moved to a 4,500 square foot home and recording studio on thirteen and a half acres in Auburn. He has had singles on the Top Ten Billboard chart and has brought national attention to Seattle as a city of new music. His first rap hit in 1985 was followed by two albums: *SWASS* in 1987 which sold a million copies, and *Seminar* in 1989 which sold 750,000 copies. Sir Mix-A-Lot has toured with several big name rap singers, and in 1992 went on a marathon two month tour of forty-five cities. His own label, **Rhyme Cartel Records,** is part of a 1992 contract with Def American Co.

After two years of research, metro engineer **Carl Mack** began marketing his *Black Heritage Day Calendar* from his Auburn home in 1992. *For information, write to him at 11521 SE 321st Place, Auburn, WA 98002, or call 206-351-9525.*

Algona and Pacific

The first African American chief of police in the state was **Al Lee** who served for five and a half months in Algona in 1983. Fourteen African Americans were living in Algona in 1990, including a policeman.

Thirty of the 4,400 residents of this fast growing town are African Americans. Most of this small group moved here after 1980. Several of them are employed by Weyerhauser or the Boeing Company.

Al Lee headed the police department in neighboring Algona prior to becoming the Chief of Police in Pacific in 1983. He is a former Marine and Washington D.C. policeman and has received commendations from officials of neighboring King County cities.

Federal Way

In 1885, **John and Mary Conna** claimed their 157 acre homestead in the Panther Lake area of Federal Way *between 334th and 10th Avenue SW and 21st Avenue SW and First Avenue South* near the Aquatic Center. Two of the five years' residency requirement for homestead ownership were met by Civil War veteran Conna's army term. In the late 1880s he became a realtor in Tacoma where a plat, **Conna Addition,** bears his name. In 1889 Conna became assistant sergeant-at-arms for the new

Washington State Senate, and sergeant-at-arms in the 1890 special session of the legislature. An ardent Republican, Mr. Conna represented the Pierce County party as a presidential elector during the convention which nominated William McKinley for President in 1896. Conna and his wife, Mary, later sold the homestead. John Conna has been mentioned by his contemporary, newspaperman Horace Cayton, as the leading lobbyist for inclusion of a public accommodations clause in Washington's first constitution.

The Conna's daughter, Katherine, married Powell Barnett, for whom a Seattle park is named. [See Central Area, Leschi Section]

Federal Way is the home of Dennis Walston, "King Limbo," who was entered in the Guiness Book of Records in 1992 for dancing under a flaming bar only six inches above the ground. He has taught classes at Federal Way's Parks and Recreation Department and performs around the county at fairs and festivals.

There has been discernible growth in the African American population of Federal Way in the last twenty years, with 2,709 counted in the 1990 census. Several small businesses, from floral arranging to computer services, are operated by members of this population. Some are located in the malls, others are home-based enterprises. Two churches advertise in the African American press in Seattle: the House of Prayer for All Nations Ministries, and the Rose of Sharon Christian Church which holds services at the Church of the Nazarene, *1525 Dash Point Road beginning at 1pm Sunday afternoons*. The Rose of Sharon was begun in 1990 by its present pastor, the Rev. M. E. Hale. *The office telephone number is 927-8131.*

Other organizations have been established in recent years, among them the Federal Way Afro-American Coalition, formed in 1992, to promote economic stability, and address social and political issues. The group meets biweekly. *For information, write P.O. Box 23204, Federal Way, WA 98093-0204.*

The Federal Way Coalition seeks to foster cultural awareness, a supportive environment, and excellence and leadership among African American youth in the area. *For meeting times and dates, call: Tacoma (206) 840-9665; or Seattle (206) 946-3678.*

Four African Americans serve on the nine-member Diversity Commission established by the City of Federal Way in 1992 to advise the City Council on issues of importance to the city's diverse population. They are: Rubi Williams, Adrian Johnson, Pam English and Arthur Cowan. *For information, call the office of the Assistant Manager Stephen Anderson, 661-4016.*

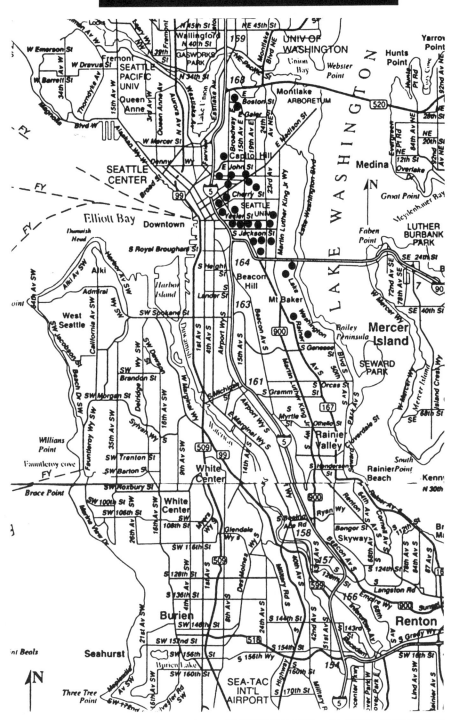

CAPITOL HILL TO MOUNT BAKER

6.
Capitol Hill to Mount Baker

Peaks and Valleys

Pioneers of various races are buried in the Lakeview Cemetery, *1500 15th Avenue E.* Among those interred here are such early African Americans as **Archy Fox,** who had a barber shop in Pioneer Square during the 1860s and 1870s; **William and Sarah Grose,** pioneer hoteliers, with the next three generations of their descendants; and **Roscoe and Theresa Brown Dixon.** Roscoe Dixon was a sometimes restaurateur and gold prospector. Theresa Dixon, was a private duty nurse who had been trained in the 1870s by the Sisters of Providence.

Across the street to the north of Lakeview is the **Grand Army of the Republic (GAR) Cemetery,** *13th Avenue and Howe Street. Approach the cemetery by traveling slowly northward from Lakeview Cemetery on 15th Avenue in order not to miss Howe, a narrow street that is not easily seen. Bus #10 ends its route near Howe.*

Civil War veterans and their families are interred in the GAR Cemetery, among them **Gideon Bailey,** who, in 1894, became one of the first African Americans in Washington to serve as justice of the peace. Bailey served three years in the army during the Civil War. He was a recruiter for the famed **54th Massachusetts Regiment** which fought for a whole year without wages to protest the government's paying a higher rate of pay to White soldiers than to African Americans.

When leaving the cemetery, head southward and turn left on Galer to reach 17th Avenue E.

Dr. Felix B. and Hazel James Cooper moved to the house at *1238 17th Avenue E. (∧)* in 1921. Felix Cooper moved to Seattle about 1914 after receiving his state certification to practice dentistry in Spokane in 1912. Hazel Cooper moved from New Zealand with her family in 1917. The family occupied the house until the 1940s. Felix B. Cooper, a graduate of the University of Michigan was a staunch member of the Mt. Zion Baptist Church, and a strong advocate of community unity and progress. He practiced dentistry in the Empire Building, at 914 Second Avenue, Downtown, for more than forty years.

The Coopers' daughter, **Joyce Cooper Arkhurst,** graduated from Garfield in 1938 and was given a trip to Brazil to visit her uncle, **Harry James,** who spent a few years in Seattle pursuing work as an architect before moving there. James designed the 1920 brick church used by the Mt. Zion Baptist congregation which was razed for the present structure in 1974. Joyce Cooper Arkhurst, a writer and librarian, was a storyteller for the New York Public Library. When she lived in Ghana, her husband's home, she heard **Anansi** stories, which she later retold and published in two children's books in 1970 and 1972.

The Anansi stories were first brought to the western hemisphere by Africans during slavery and became the basis of Joel Chandler Harris's *Uncle Remus Stories.*

Return to 15th Avenue and head south, turning right at Roy Street.

African American association with **Cornish College of the Arts,** *710 East Roy,* dates to the school's early days. Theodosia Young remembers Miss "Aunt" Nellie Cornish, the founder of this school, as a friend of her mother's, gallery owner **Zoe Dusanne,** during the 1920s. **Syvilla Fort,** dancer and teacher, was a student here in the 1930s when she met composer John Cage and choreographer Merce Cunningham. Cage, in trying to accommodate Fort's need for a variety of percussion instruments on the school's small stage with her need for dancing space, devised an arrangement which evolved into his famous "prepared piano." Nationally known jazz trombonist **Julian Priester** teaches at Cornish, as does photographer and painter **Preston Wadley.** Priester's wife, Nashira, is a set decorator for theatrical films.

Remain on Roy, travel eastward and turn right onto Broadway.

The **Broadway Market,** *431 Broadway E.,* is where you will find **Uzuri,** *323-3238,* a shop with a wide range of items from the eastern coast of Africa, ranging from cloth to carvings. On the first level of the market are pushcart vendors, among them **40 Acres and a Mule,** which specializes in clothing and accessories with themes from African American life, inspired by the work of film-maker Spike Lee.

Other Seattle High Points

Most of the old Broadway High School, and its successor in the building, **Edison Technical School,** were levelled in the 1970s, leaving only the skeleton of the structure now called the Broadway Performance Hall. **Marita Harris,** one of the first two African American teachers in Seattle, began her Seattle career at Edison Tech. where she taught home economics courses. The president of the college, **Dr. Charles Mitchell,** was chosen in 1987, after six years as Dean of Student Personnel Services at the college. He succeeded **Dr. Donald Phelps,** who served as president from 1980 to 1984 when he became chancellor of the Seattle Community College District before he resigned to head the Los Angeles Community College District in 1988.

The lot north of the bookstore intended for the Student Activities Center is the site of **Stone's Silver Catering Service and Confectionery,** a luxury silver shop and Ben and Jerry's rolled into one. This business was operated by **Samuel Stone** from the 1910s to the 1930s. Older residents recall that the complete serviceware used by the owners to cater banquets and special dinners in the homes of the county's well-to-do citizenry was of sterling silver. Mr. Stone's ice cream is reputed to have been without parallel in Seattle and its environs.

Poet and writer **J. T. Stewart** teaches writing courses at the college. Actress and dramatist **Tawnya Pettiford-Waites** is on the drama faculty. **Nate Long,** former Hollywood stunt man, and Emmy Award nominee who directed *South By Northwest,* a made-for-television series on the 19th century history of African Americans in the Northwest, is lead instructor of the college's Arts and Applied Technology program.

In 1984, sociology instructor **Rosetta Hunter,** who came to the college in 1971, was appointed chair of the Humanities and Social Sciences division of the college. Hunter has served as faculty advisor to the **Pan Afrikan Student Union.** Another sociology instructor, **Gilda Sheppard,** began studies in Ghana for a doctorate in anthropology in 1992. The work of African American artists is shown in the college's gallery at the north end of the atrium.

The college also houses the Middle College High School which serves over two hundred students, over half of them of African descent. **Dr. Alice V. Houston,** director of staff development for the Seattle Public Schools, founded this school in collaboration with Seattle Housing Authority, SCCC and CITICORP in 1990 to serve high school dropouts.

In 1989, **Dr. Carver Gayton** was named by Governor Gardner as a replacement for attorney **Phillip Burton,** longtime civil rights advocate, who had served as a trustee of the Seattle Community Colleges Board for many years. The board oversees operations of the Community College District. Gayton, a Seattle native and former teacher, at the time of his appointment, was a member of the University of Washington's College of

Arts and Sciences Development Board, and has served on numerous other boards.

The office of The Gable Design Group, *400 East Pine Street, 329-4742,* is west of the college. Former Boeing graphic designer Tony Gable formed the group in 1985, and it has since produced award-winning designs and promotional packages for businesses around the country. The signature dancing man symbolizing Festival Sundiata was created by this group.

Architect Donald I. King and Associates, *323-7749,* has offices at *1700 Bellevue.* The firm was begun in 1985 by Donald King, formerly the principal architect of Environmental Works. It provides services from consulting, to planning and design. King graduated with a B.F.A. in Interior Architecture in 1975 from Wayne State University in Detroit, and three years later with a Master of Architecture degree from UCLA. He is on the Seattle Planning Commission and teaches Architectural Drafting at SCCC. Lauri Wilson, an associate of the firm, is a founding member of the Minority and Women Architects Association, which sponsors the Architects in the Schools Program.

Two blocks south of the college old Firehouse #25 stands on part of the block owned by William Hedges who acquired more property than any other African American in Seattle during the 1860s and 1870s. This block, bordered by Pike and Union, Broadway and Harvard, sold for four hundred and forty dollars upon Hedges's death in 1871.

Twelfth Avenue Interlude
Retrace your steps to reach Pike, and go east to 12th Avenue to reach the old Woodson apartments, at the northeast corner of 12th Avenue and Pike Street.

Most of the buildings erected by African Americans in King County were designed by master builders or carpenters rather than architects. One of the most accomplished builders was Robert Butler who came to Seattle in the 1890s. About 1905, he and another African American, a man named Tibbs, built this apartment building for Zacharias and Irene Woodson who moved from Chicago in 1897. Many African Americans found accommodations at this building upon arrival in Seattle during the early years of the century. In a 1909 Seattle *Republican* article, Butler was reported to have built more houses in Seattle than any other African American.

Some people come here just to go to Fergie's Cheesecake Plus, *1204 East Pike Street, 328-1724,* for extraordinary renditions of two African American favorites, peach cobbler and sweet potato pie—prepared as cheese-cakes! Of course, there's the plain-old delicious, standard cheesecake for the less adventuresome, as well. This is primarily a wholesale operation, but a few tables accommodate walk-in customers. The owner is friendly, and the coffee good.

Continue southward on 12th Avenue for about two blocks to reach **Kokeb Ethiopian Restaurant,** *926 12th Avenue.* It is the oldest continental African food restaurant in the county. Established in the early 1980s, this restaurant offers typical Ethiopian food and live Ethiopian music on the weekends and during special holidays. In 1989 Kokeb was voted one of the three best ethnic restaurants in the city.

A few doors south of the restaurant stands the old **"908" Club** which in the 1920s was the place to see and be seen. It was lavishly appointed throughout, featuring expensive Oriental rugs, liveried doormen and uniformed waitpersons, excellent dishes, some of the best jazz, and indisputably the best barbeque in town. The owner's own "New Orleans Gin Fizz" was a popular choice.

The "908" was built in 1926 by **John Henry "Doc" Hamilton,** a Mississippian who was among the group of southerners recruited by **Alfred Roberts,** to work on construction of the streets of Victoria, B. C. In Victoria, Hamilton was tutored in foot care by an African Canadian podiatrist by the name of Jones. Thus the nickname "Doc" Hamilton which was given him in the Canadian army where he treated Canadian officers' feet. He moved to Seattle prior to World War I, and later served in the United States army. After his discharge from the army in 1919, Doc returned to Seattle

The former "908" Club as it appeared in 1935.
(King County Regional Archives)

and operated nightclubs, cabarets and roadhouses in several smaller locations until he was able to erect this building.

In the early 1930s, Doc was sentenced to prison on a charge growing out of his permitting gambling in the back rooms of the establishment. He had made many friends through his business, but his downfall is reported to have come about at the instigation of two powerful White businessmen whose wrath he incurred when he asked them to leave after they became intoxicated to an obnoxious degree.

From there events took a rapid turn downhill, ending a few days later in a raid on the house, and Doc being charged with illegally operating gambling activities on the premises. Oral history sources have confided that there was indeed gambling on the premises, but that the tables were run by a woman who sub-leased the space. Doc Hamilton, however, took the rap, and was sentenced to a prison term at Walla Walla. He was able to salvage a shred of his dignity by notifying the sentencing judge that he would drive himself to prison, and he did! Unbelievable as it seems, he arrived at Walla Walla earlier than he was expected, and had to wait at the prison gate a couple of hours before being admitted.

In 1939 he tried to reopen the "908," but the Depression had permanently changed the entertainment scene. People were no longer able to spend lavishly, and the "908's" duration was short. From his own recipe he bottled and sold to hotels and restaurants "Doc Hamilton's Barbecue Sauce" which provided a modest income for him during his lean years. He died in poverty in an International District hotel in 1942.

A few businesses along 12th Avenue suggest a slight resemblance to the area near Jackson at an earlier time of pronounced commercial activity among African Americans.

In 1950, **Charles Stokes**, *452 12th Avenue*, was the first African American in King County to be elected to the Washington State Legislature, and the third in the history of the state. Stokes, a native of Fredonia, Kansas, has been a Seattle resident since 1943. He was appointed Judge in the County District Court in 1968, and re-elected continuously until his retirement in 1978 when he resumed the practice of law.

The structure at *319 12th Avenue* is the former **Angelus Funeral Home Building.** From 1930 until 1977 African Americans owned this building which housed a business begun during World War I at a time of expanded economic activity among African Americans.

Continue southward on 12th to Jackson Street. You may continue eastward on Jackson to explore up to 23rd, or continue along 12th to Beacon Hill. The #14 Mt. Baker bus travels the length of Jackson and may be taken

*near the southeast corner of the intersection. Buses #36 and #60 turn onto
12th Avenue and travel to Beacon Hill.*

At the *southeast corner of the intersection of 12th and Jackson* stands a
one story brick building which formerly housed the **Black and Tan** nightclub, an after-hours club which was known coast to coast for its superb
jam sessions. It was a favorite gathering place for local musicians as well as
famous visiting artists traveling the theater circuits. Musicians such as **Duke
Ellington, Sarah Vaughn, Louis Armstrong,** and Lionel Hampton came
to the club to play sets after performing in downtown performance halls.

The buildings at this corner, and those which formerly occupied the half
block directly across the street at the northeast corner, were owned by
Russell "Noodles" Smith, a well-known sporting figure in Seattle in the
first part of the 20th century.

Smith came to Seattle about 1907, after parlaying five dollars into seventeen thousand dollars in a weekend of gambling at Goldfield, Nevada.
The origin of his nickname "Noodles" remains a mystery. He was a hard-
headed businessman, tireless worker for the rehabilitation of young African American men who had been in prison, and a philanthropist. A local
newspaper reported in his obituary that he supported fifty families during

Black and Tan Orchestra, about 1928.
(Courtesy Robert Wright)

the Great Depression of the 1930s, although much of his philanthropy was performed anonymously.

Smith operated the Golden West Hotel which once stood at *710 7th Avenue*, and the Coast Hotel at *9th and King* , which was demolished for the construction of the I- 5 Freeway. After the 1930s Smith retired from the hotel business, but he operated the Ubangi nightclub with its African decor and lavish floor show and revue at the old Golden West at the same time he operated the Little Harlem nightclub and cabaret, and the Black and Tan. During the late '20s and '30s, Smith's uptown Little Harlem Club broadcast a short jazz program to radio cabs tuned to a certain frequency.

Smith had an amicable relationship with the Downtown establishment until the 1926 election of Seattle's first female mayor, reform candidate Bertha Landes. In fact, some of the downtown businessmen are said to have frequented his place. Up until the election he had operated gaming tables at the Golden West, often for high stakes. But the reformed-minded mayor soon began cracking down on such activities, and his business was raided repeatedly. Declaring that he was "not going to work for that old woman," he shut down the tables, and he never had any use for the "lady mayor."

Celebration and Enterprise

A small district of African American businesses burgeoned in the area in the 1910s as are Asian American businesses today. So vibrant was the area in 1919, that newspaperman Horace Cayton compared it to Chicago's State Street and Beale Street in Memphis. I. I. Walker opened his hotel in the 1000 block of Jackson Street after returning from eleven years in the Yukon Territory. The Alhambra Cash Grocery was located at *1036-38-40 Jackson Street,* now the parking lot for the Asian Plaza. In 1916 it advertised "a select line of staple and fancy groceries," and promised "auto delivery to any part of the city." Its owners Harry Legg and W. H. Banks bought from local growers such favored African foods as collard greens, and imported yams and watermelons from the South and a few Washington State sources to please their African American customers. From World War I until the late 1930s they sponsored the Alhambra baseball team.

African Americans lived, and operated small businesses, in what is now the International District from the late 1880s. The businesses ranged from itinerant sandwich sellers to employment offices. In the 1950s, others opened shop on Jackson. Charles Adams operated a tailoring shop at Sixth and Jackson until his death in 1977; Bishops' Drugstore was a fixture for over thirty years; Pat and Irma Francis operated their dry cleaning business for over twenty years on Jackson near Maynard; and Franglor's, now on First Avenue S., opened at Maynard and Jackson in the 1970s. **Dussie Jackson** ran her **Jackson's Diner** at the location of the International District Post Office in the 1950s. Her son, **Andrew,** was an accounting intern at the Wing Luke Museum in 1992.

Keith Godfrey Johnson who, as a young man found his dreams of becoming an engineer thwarted by the Depression, operated a barbershop in the Atlas Hotel from the mid-forties until the 1960s. He devised a miniature clipper attachment for a special styling technique. In spite of a patent, a national razor company to which he unsuccessfully proposed sale of the idea later marketed an attachment which was remarkably similar to Johnson's device. One of Johnson's daughters, **Anita Connell,** is an obstetrician.

As you travel eastward along Jackson you notice a small peninsula occupied by a Vietnamese restaurant at the intersection of 14th and Jackson with Rainier and Boren. This was **Neversleep's** corner. He was an easily recognizable Seattle character with an amputated arm, and a foghorn voice, who hawked newspapers all hours of the day and late into the night. Legend has it that his arm was lost when he had to make a choice between losing it or losing his life after his mackinaw sleeve caught in lumber mill

East Union-East Madison Seafair Parade Float, about 1950.
(Al Smith)

machinery which was pulling him to his death. As **Robert Wright**, the late nephew of "Noodles" Smith, remembered it, "Neversleep" hacked off his arm with a hatchet when he realized that he could not extricate himself from the coat in time to avoid the blades of the giant saws.

Zion Preparatory Academy and Daycare Center, *620 20th Avenue S.*, is located in the old St. Mary's Roman Catholic School Building. This kindergarten through eighth grade school was founded on religious principles in 1982 by the **Rev. and Mrs. Eugene Drayton** of the **Zion United House of Prayer**. Students, wearing their school uniforms, come from all parts of the county. In addition to regular academic courses students participate in a horticultural class taught by **Nolan Booty**, who formerly painted portraits in Pike Place Market and now lives in Kitsap County. Booty continues to paint and his work is exhibited in galleries around the Sound and is in private collections nationwide. He is also a collector of African American memorabilia. The Booty family grows flowers which are sold in the market.

For more than a dozen years the park, *between Dearborn and Judkins*, has been the site of the annual **Black Community Festival** which began in 1971 as an outgrowth of the **East Madison-East Union Seafair Mardi Gras Parade and Festival**, one of the oldest in the city.

Drive south of Zion Academy on 20th Avenue to approach Judkins Park from Judkins Street. Walkers may enter the park from Dearborn Street, Nye Place and South Charles Street, or from 23rd Avenue S. when traveling along that thoroughfare.

During the 1990-91 school year students at Washington Middle School, *2101 South Jackson*, under the supervision of the school's art teacher, Jane Morris, painted the mural on the wall bordering the school's driveway.

On the site of the Seattle Vocational Institute, *315 22nd Avenue S.*, the **Cayton** family bought an apartment building after loss of their large Capitol Hill house following a controversial public accommodations suit and damaging testimony introduced against Horace Cayton in 1915. This was the first home of several of the families who date their coming to Seattle to the years of World War I. The building was later sold to Ms. **Cephas** who named it the **Charlena**, after one of her daughters, Charlena Mace, who lives in Seattle. The frame building was replaced with the present building which was constructed in 1967 for the Seattle Opportunities

Industrialization Center. In 1988 the state purchased the building and began vocational classes in it. .

On the same side of the street on the next corner is "Momma's," a combination restaurant-rescue station operated by Gerthaline Jackson. For the first time that anyone could remember Momma's was closed for three days in late summer of 1992. During that time over one hundred people from businesses, churches and service organizations volunteered to clean, repair, install shelving, paint the restaurant and refurbish its furnishings. Jackson is back to her routine of dispensing burgers and love to those who come to her place. Neighborhood children stop by after school, and sometimes before, and always receive a kind word and something to eat here, often without pay. Hamburgers and soul food are standard fare.

On the east (exterior) wall of the restaurant building is a mural on AIDS prevention which was painted by neighborhood children in Pratt Center art classes in 1990.

Continue across 23rd Avenue following the Jackson Street tour [see Central Area], or head two blocks north to Yesler. You may reverse the Central Area tour here, or reverse a portion of the Jackson Street tour, working your way back to 12th Avenue.

Yesler Shows the Way

At Yesler, begin your tour with the Catholic Community Services, southeast corner of 23rd and Yesler, where you may view the Eddie Walker murals, during regular operating hours, then head east to Leschi School, 135 32nd Avenue, to view the artwork of local children.

One of the goals of the Leschi Improvement Council's Neighborhood Plan was a playground which the Seattle Park Department acquired just east of the Leschi school. When seven year old Peppi Braxton was killed by a car in 1971, Leschi students decided to dedicate the small park to his memory. The wall of bas reliefs at the southwest corner of Leschi was designed by architect Leon Bridges and the students in 1963.

Return to Yesler, and head westward to explore the rest of the street.

The residence at *116 25th Avenue* (∿), is the former home of Gordon and Nella Carter. Gordon Carter was a stationary engineer. Nella Carter, a graduate of Tuskegee, received her masters in public health nursing from the UW in 1928. She was the first African American in the county to be employed as a social worker, and the first to receive a nursing degree from the UW.

The **Douglass-Truth Library** [See Central Area]

The **Odessa Brown Clinic,** *2101 East Yesler Way,* is named in honor of a community volunteer who was one of the organizers of the Central Area Motivation Program, the Madrona Block Club, and the Model City Health Task Force which worked faithfully for the establishment of the clinic prior to her death from leukemia in 1969.

Established in 1970 as part of the Model Cities Program, this clinic is, in many ways, a tribute to **Dr. Blanche Lavizzo,** a clinic founder and first medical director, who out of her concern for children of the working poor, and in conjunction with community residents, convinced Children's Hospital and Medical Center and the city, of the need for a clinic in the Central Area. Since her death in 1984, the clinic has continued Dr. Lavizzo's philosophy of providing quality care with dignity. Satellite clinics in Bellevue and Renton are built upon the success of the Odessa Brown Clinic.

The clinic was first housed at the **Cherry Hill Building,** *1700 East Cherry,* before moving to the former Herzl Synagogue, near Yesler. Since 1985, the clinic has sponsored an annual *Martin Luther King, Jr./Blanche S. Lavizzo Lecture* in February, which is free to the community. The clinic sponsors a free storytelling series which is held every fourth Thursday. Near the entry way is *My Testament in Stone,* a three ton stone sculpture by **James Washington, Jr.** which was dedicated in 1981. It was funded by the King County Arts Commission, with support from the Children's Hospital and the Seattle Arts Commission.

In 1989 Odessa Brown, **Carolyn Downs Family Medical Center,** and the Seattle-King County Health Department began discussions on expanding services and

Former Seattle architect Leon Bridges.

new programs from a Central Area health care campus at one site. In later discussions the Odessa Brown site was determined to be large enough to accommodate the clinics and office space for all three. **Donald King and Associates** are co-architects for the design of the building's exterior.

The Odessa Brown building at this site stands just west of the old **Volume Food Basket,** a cooperative supermarket which was built and operated by African Americans in the late 1950s and succeeded by two other cooperative grocery stores, the **Black Front Grocery** and later the **Serve-U Market.**

A block north of the clinic is the **New Hope Baptist Church,** *124 21st Avenue, 323-4212,* which was designed by **Ben McAdoo.** Under the leadership of its pastor, the **Rev. Robert Jeffrey,** the church's progressive outreach program spearheads the **Black Dollar Days** Task Force *(323-4212),* which publishes the **Black Business Directory.** The church also co-sponsors the Inner City Entrepreneurial Training Program held on its premises, and hosts some South Africa support activities.

Plans were announced by a committee headed by Mrs. Toby Burton and Dr. Abraham Bergman in 1992 to create a **Dr. Blanche Lavizzo Children's Play Area,** a "living memorial," with an African theme, in Pratt Park, Main and Yesler, *between 19th Avenue and 20th Avenue.*

Edwin Pratt was executive director of the **Seattle Urban League** at the time of his assassination in 1970. Mr. Pratt was a tireless and vocal fighter for open housing, fair employment practices, integrated schools and an end to police brutality. In the southwest corner of the **Edward Pratt Park,** is the **Pratt Fine Arts Center,** *1902 South Main,* where a variety of art forms are taught by professionals including the painter Samaj. Much of the children's art on bus shelters and buildings in the area is by young Pratt students. The center presents an annual Edwin T. Pratt Memorial Exhibit featuring local African American artists each February.

In the middle of the blockas you travel westward, is the aptly-named **R. & L. Home of Good Barbecue** at *1816 Yesler Way, 322-0271,* which has been dispensing some of the best barbecue in the county for more than twenty years. Diners may eat at the restaurant, but most of the business is carry-out. *Closed Sundays and Mondays.*

Across the street from the restaurant is **Bryant Manor,** a large apartment building which belongs to the **First African Methodist Episcopal Church,** and provides housing for families of moderate income.

The **Langston Hughes Cultural Arts Center,** *104 17th Avenue S., 625-5357,* was founded in 1972. Housed in a former synagogue, the center provides a variety of activities including dance and cultural offerings from the **Shona** people of Zimbabwe taught by Zimbabwean **Lora Chiora Dye,** music and dance of the **Dan** people of Liberia, and occasionally capoeira, self-defense choreography from Africa by way of Brazil. This is the former home of the **Paul Robeson Performing Arts Company.** The **Madrona Theatre,** a youth performing arts company, is housed here. **Chipupugwendere,** an annual African Harvest Festival, and occasional **Kwanza** celebrations are also held here. The African Writers' Association meets here monthly.

Pansy's Restaurant, *1715 East Yesler Way, 325-0293,* is open for breakfast and lunch, Monday through Friday. This very leisurely-paced restaurant offers some of the best smothered chicken available in the county. It also provides catering service.

The **Goodwill Missionary Baptist Church,** *126th 15th Avenue,* was designed by **Leon Bridges,** who entered practice in architecture in 1963. The church's outreach includes operation of a home for single mothers.

Since its founding in 1930, the **Urban League of Seattle,** *105 14th Avenue, 461-3792,* has had offices in a variety of places. It now occupies its own building, the old St. George hotel. Under its current director, **Dr. Rosalind Woodhouse,** the league has expanded the number of innovative programs to address educational needs, employment opportunities, and parenting skills. One of its most-publicized activities is the annual November art exhibition which, since its beginning in 1977, has introduced scores of artists of color to the public. Dr. Woodhouse was one of the first two African Americans to receive appointment as head of a state office when she was appointed in 1980 to head the Department of Licensing.

"A Taste of Blackness" is the latest custom-designed cruise offered by **Pizazz Travel,** *300 14th Avenue S., 322-1987; 1-800-55-CLASS,* in conjunction with the Urban League Affiliates. Pizazz, begun in 1982, provides regular travel services, and specializes in vacation and group travel tours to Bermuda, Mexico and the Caribbean.

Many of the students at Bailey Gatzert Elementary School, *1301 East Yesler,* are African American or Asian American, several of them from nearby Yesler Terrace Housing. The entire student body participated in the dedication of one of James Washington, Jr.'s latest sculptures, *Touchstone With Eagles,* in 1991.

The Coming of the Purifiers, on the wall of the King County Records Warehouse at *13th and Yesler,* is one of the largest murals in the city. It was painted during the summer of 1977 by muralist Don Barrie with the assistance of twenty community participants in the city's Summer Youth Employment Program who were paid three dollars an hour. The work was commissioned by the King County Arts Commission, with support from the Urban League, former County Executive John Spellman, Local 76 of the

Musicians' Association, KING television, the Pacific Science Center, and Battalion Three of the Seattle Fire Department.

At the corner of *12th Avenue, Yesler and Boren* is **Lloyd's Rocket Fuel.** It was established in 1970 by **Joseph Lloyd** after he borrowed $60,000 from the Small Business Administration and the former Liberty Bank to buy this old-fashioned gas station, one of a very few left in the county. Over the years the station provided full repair and fuel service, and Lloyd delivered home heating oil in a two thousand gallon tanker truck that is usually parked near the station. He has rented the garage section to Vietnamese refugees, and now rents to Ethiopian refugees.

In 1939, after a survey revealed that more than a quarter of the city's housing was substandard, the Seattle City Council voted to establish the Seattle Housing Authority. Yesler Terrace, bordered by I-5, Boren, Washington, and Jefferson, was the Authority's response. The 868 original housing units were reduced to 602, following the construction of I-5. About one third of the residents here are of African descent, including several families from the Horn of Africa. In 1987 former public housing resident **Harry Thomas** became head of the housing authority. He was appointed Governor Mike Lowry's Chief of Staff in 1993.

Neighborhood House, an outgrowth of Jewish resettlement efforts beginning in the early twentieth century, offers a wide range of services to Yesler Terrace residents. It is headed by urban planner **Alfred Poole**, a former resident. The community council has secured a bus route and a greenhouse for the residents, eliminated brazen drug trafficking, and sponsors an annual **"Juneteenth" Celebration**, and a program recognizing graduates of middle and senior high school and college.

The community center, under supervision of **Pat Warburg** and **Arthur Banks**, provides a number of activities for the children, some of which have earned city-wide recognition. The art students have had public showings at Seattle University and the Pacific Arts Center. Their work decorates the bus shelter at Broadway and Yesler. Sculptor **Charles Paris**, whose work may be seen at **Maison Bleu Gallery**, lives here.

Creation and Remembrance
The #9 bus traveling southward may be taken from Yesler Terrace to reach Beacon Hill via Boren, or the #36 bus may be taken from 12th Avenue and Jackson Street.

Immigrants of African descent have lived in the county since the first days of settlement and added to the cultural mix with cuisine, religion, and literary and artistic contributions. One of the most stunning art forms to arrive in recent years is that of theatrical carnival art. The most seasoned and gifted practitioner in the county is Fitzgerald De Freitas of De Freitas Creations, who works in his home at *1337 14th Avenue S. (325-2994)*. A master creator of costumes and props, De Freitas has worked with children and adult novices in recreating this exciting expression of celebration in his native Trinidad.

Small numbers of African Americans have resided on, or owned property, in the tracts south of Jackson since the middle of the nineteenth century. In 1869, George Riley, president of the Workingmen's Joint Stock Association of Portland, Oregon purchased for two thousand dollars in gold coin, the four blocks on Beacon Hill which are now bounded by South Forest and South Lander Streets, between 19th Avenue and 21st Avenue S. Two years later the corporation purchased the eight additional blocks bounded by South Lander and South Stevens Streets and 17th Avenue and 20th Avenue. [See end of Downtown section]

In the 1880s, several families resided on 11th Avenue S. One of the residents, Brittain Oxendine, was publisher of the Seattle *Standard*, the first African American newspaper in King County, which was begun in 1891. The house at *2709 21st Avenue S. (⋏)* was built and occupied in 1911 by George Wright, grandson of George Riley, president of the WJSA whose name is on the Kroll plat map of Seattle used by the County Assessor's Office today.

Chiropodists James and Letitia Graves lived in several places after their arrival in Seattle in 1906. They were living in the house at *2716 21st Avenue S. (⋏)*, in 1915 when their daughter Zola Mae Young, later known as Zoe Dusanne, moved to Seattle with her young daughter.

On 21st Avenue South head northward, turn right onto Walker Street, crossing Rainier Avenue and Martin Luther King Way South.

At the southeast corner of MLK and Walker is the Martin Luther King Memorial. The idea of a monument originated with Seattle resident Charlie James in 1983, and was taken up by a multi-racial committee which held a ground-breaking in 1984, but languished as time passed.

An African American committee was formed later, composed of Dr. Samuel Kelly, brother of the sculptor, Robert Kelly, the Rev. Samuel McKinney, Bill McIntosh, Freddie Mae Gautier, and Herman McKinney, with sponsorship of Central Area Motivation Project. The City of Seattle made $130,000 available from Block Grant funds to clear, grade and plant grass at the 4.7 acre site. The movement was advanced when King County included twenty-five thousand dollars in its 1988 budget to hire a full-time

Martin Luther King, Jr.
Memorial
(Office of
Senator Dwight Pelz)

director of fund-raising for the effort. A grant was also received from the King County Arts Commission. In 1991, the State Legislature appropriated $100,000 towards completion of the work.

The thirty-foot high black Zimbabwean granite monument, symbolizing Dr. King's "I've been to the mountaintop" speech was designed by **Robert W. Kelly**, an Edmonds Community College instructor. **Avent Technologies, Inc.**, headed by engineer **Roy A. Avent**, provided the design and construction for the monument. The reflecting pool is surrounded by plaques bearing significant events in Dr. King's life. Inscribed donor bricks, which were purchased for fifty dollars each, pave an area in back of the monument. A donor's wall provides special recognition for donors of five hundred dollars or more. The monument was dedicated November 16, 1991. At the dedication ceremony, twelve Idaho Pink Locust trees donated by First Interstate Bank were planted by TREEmendous Seattle. The **Martin Luther King, Jr.** national holiday is observed on the third Monday of January. El Centro de la Raza, *2524 16th Avenue S., 329-2974,* offers an annual course on the philosophy of Dr. King through their Community University King Resource Center.

Martin Luther King, Jr. Way became the official name of the former Empire Way, an eight mile street in Seattle in 1982, following a long struggle for the name change which was led by Seattle businessman, and former

CAMP head, **Eddie Rye.** That portion of the street extending outside of the city retained the original name.

Mount Baker District

Continue eastward on Walker to reach the Mount Baker District. Turn left onto 31st Avenue S. and drive to Atlantic Street. The #14 bus travels the length of 31st Avenue S.

St. Clement's Episcopal Church *(1501 32nd Avenue S.)* celebrated its one hundredth anniversary in 1991. This small gem of a church was originally organized by a middle-class White congregation. Its first African American family, nurse **Theresa Brown Dixon** and two of her children **Mabel** and **Chester Dixon,** joined in 1899. In 1926, **St. Phillips,** an African American mission in the East Madison district was sponsored by St. Clement's. Since its move to the Mt. Baker district in 1948, St. Clement's has become the most thoroughly integrated Episcopal church in western Washington, (more than fifty percent of its enrolled members are African American, down from about seventy-five percent in the early 1970s) absorbing many of the members of the **Church of the Advent,** a primarily African American congregation which grew out of St. Phillip's Mission.

St Clement's celebrates its diversity by a handsome altar frontal of Kente cloth, Indian silk, and English damask, executed by its pastor, the Rev. Fr. **Ralph Carskadden,** an artist and former textile dealer of Swedish ancestry. Among the saints and icons in the church are **St. Moses of Egypt and Ethiopia,** an African Christ by a South African artist, and icons of **Absolom Jones** and **Martin Luther King.** Its worship service includes use of the hymnal *Lift Every Voice and Sing,* which contains traditional spirituals and hymns.

The Church's Centennial cookbook has a large section on southern cookery, much of it drawn from its African American members. A small Martin Luther King library is developing, and photographs of women honored by the Churchwomen of the parish are displayed in the undercroft. *Call ahead to see the church (324-3072) or visit Sunday services at 10am.*

St. Clement's is home to the **Sounds of the Northwest,** an *a capella* choir founded in 1987 by **Juan Huey-Ray,** which specializes in traditional spirituals. Ray is assistant music conductor at First African Methodist Episcopal Church.

Ollie Taylor has been a continuous supplier of Gospel sheet music, records, tapes, information and supplies since she opened **Ollie's Gospel Corner,** *1400 31st Avenue S.,* 329-8742, in 1976. She began broadcasting gospel music that year on KBLE radio, and has the longest career of any gospel disc jockey in the country. She was interviewed by the Smithsonian Institution in 1992 regarding her broadcasting experience, the first field work the Smithsonian had conducted on gospel music in Washington State. Her customers come from Canada to Portland. Gospel concerts are also held at the Gospel Corner. The True Vine of Holiness Pentecostal Church, pastored by the Rev. J. Huggins, meets at the hall on Sunday mornings. *Taylor's program Heaven Bound Train is broadcast on KRIZ 1420 AM, Sundays 5-10am. Ollie's Gospel Corner is open Monday-Saturday.*

Drive north on 31st Avenue to Judkins and turn right. At 32nd, turn left.

Mildred German was the first African American school social worker in King County. She began work in the Seattle Public Schools a year after her arrival from North Carolina in 1949. As Director of Curriculum Development for Title I in Seattle Public Schools in 1968 she headed the multiracial curriculum committee which produced *The Role of Racial Minorities in the United States, a Resource Book for Seattle Teachers* (Seattle Public Schools). She lived in the house at *1124 32nd Avenue S.* (∿) for more than thirty years.

Return to Judkins, turn right to reach 31st and head north for one block, turning left at Norman Street.

Thelma Dewitty was one of the first two teachers of African descent hired by the Seattle Public School District. (The other was **Marita Johnson Harris** who taught at Edison Technical School.) Dewitty applied to teach while she was a teacher in Corpus Christi, Texas and a summer graduate student studying mathematics at the University of Washington in 1947, the year she was hired. At the time of her death in 1977, Dewitty was working on a mathematics textbook. Dewitty was active in the campaign for a Washington State Fair Employment Practices law. She resided at *1101 S. Yakima Place at Norman Street* (∿) for many years.

Return to 31st Avenue, turning right to head south. Turn left at Bayview to reach 34th Avenue S.

The residence at *2540 34th Ave. S.* (∿) was the home of **Frazier Augustus Boutelle**, army officer and conservationist, and his wife **Mary Haydon Boutelle**. Frazier Boutelle entered the military during the Civil War serving first as a cavalryman, and then in the ambulance corps. He was discharged at the end of the war, but reenlisted in 1866. In 1890, he was recommended for brevet major. In this rank he served as an adjutant, a recruiter, and as an inspector of National Guard units before his appointment as the superintendent of Yellowstone National Park. Boutelle retired from the army in 1897, but served as an army recruiter in Seattle from 1905 to 1918. Mary Boutelle lived in the house until the late 1930s.

In addition to having some of the county's loveliest homes, Mount Baker is graced with **Franklin High School** which is visible at the end of 31st Avenue. It is a National Register of Historic Places, and a city of Seattle, Landmark. Franklin is one of the most impressive architectural treasures of the south end. The school, with a student body approximately thirty percent African American, reopened in 1991 after a complete renovation and restoration.

Among the five artworks sponsored by the Seattle School District and the Art in Public Places Program of the Washington State Arts Commission, as part of the public art phase of the renovation, are four ten-foot tall "totem figures," a monumental installment by Auburn artist **Marita Dingus.** Composed of artifacts used at the school since its opening in 1912, it is located on the second floor, just outside the school's library. This sculpture is considerably larger than Ms. Dingus' usual format.

Mount Baker is one of the county's most diverse neighborhoods, economically and racially. This was not always the case. Although the name is applied to a greatly expanded territory today, it was originally platted by the Hunter Tract Improvement Company as a residential area for those the company defined as the "best people" in a smaller area embracing the Mt. Baker Park neighborhood. Persons of African descent were not included in this category by the developers and the first purchasers. Within a year of its opening lots for public sale however, two discrimination suits were brought to open the area to all persons with the necessary means of purchase. One of these was **Susie Stone,** whose husband, Samuel, operated **Stone's Silver Catering Service** on Broadway. [See Capitol Hill section]

With the growth in Seattle's population after 1900, African Americans found an increasing number of informal, and after 1923, formal, restrictions raised against their purchasing property. Those with means and fortitude resorted to a number of measures to circumvent the restrictions: lawsuits; purchase by light-skinned family members and friends; purchases by Whites; and after World War II, in at least one case, by a Japanese person, who then sold it to the African American purchaser.

Susie Stone, noting that one African American in 1909 had brought a discrimination suit against the developers, purchased a lot through a White intermediary. Relying on the adage that "what one woman can't do, two can," she and the buyer worked out an arrangement. Upon her final payment, Stone proceeded to claim her deed for the property. The developers, however, contended that Stone was not the kind of buyer they had in mind, and refused to relinquish the deed. But they underestimated the tenacity of Stone, who, with the assistance of **Andrew Black,** a determined **Howard University** and New York Law School graduate, challenged the recalcitrant developers at all levels, with the courts ruling in their favor. But it was not until 1911, two years later, following a favorable state Supreme Court ruling, that Susie and Samuel Stone were able to build the house on the disputed lot at *3125 34th Avenue S.* (*N*).

Andrew Black came to Seattle in 1901 and assumed the work begun in the county in 1891 by earlier lawyers who challenged discriminatory practices. He died in the influenza epidemic of 1918.

Mount Baker is also home to Seattle's first mayor of African descent, the Honorable **Norman B. Rice,** and his family. Prior to his election to the City Council for three terms, and as mayor in 1990, Mr. Rice served as president of the Mount Baker Community Club, an organization dating to 1912.

MADISON STREET

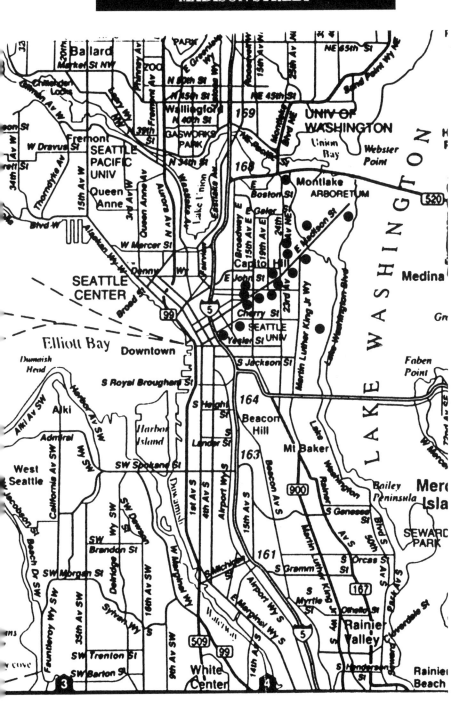

7.
Madison Street

A Slice of the Central District, Route 1
To begin this tour from the north, cross the Mountlake Bridge, take the Lake Washington Boulevard turnoff to the Museum of History and Industry. Visit the museum en route.

View the Callahan mural panels in the auditorium, part of a larger WPA-sponsored mural which includes Black and White stevedores. The first Holiday Festival of Black Dolls, *P.O. Box 1212, Bellevue, WA 98709-1212, 643-4154,* now an annual affair, was held here in 1983 by its founder LaVerne Hall, a Bellevue resident. The festival is the nation's oldest and largest traveling Black doll festival. It has been held in Oakland, Topeka, Houston, Dallas, and Wilberforce, Ohio. In the early 1980s, Hall, a dollmaker and paper doll artist, founded the Carter G. Woodson Group to preserve and promote African American history.

The art of Isaac Shamsud-Din, Portland artist and cultural worker, was exhibited in *Isaac Shamsud-Din: Public and Personal Work,* which was featured at the museum in the spring of 1980.

Gallery of Greats, a 1986 exhibit of the work of Colorado Springs artist Clarence Shivers was held here. In 1989, Dr. Edward Jones, retired lecturer at the University of Washington, presented his drama based on ancient African history here. Dr. Jones has authored several books on Africans in antiquity.

In 1991 the museum hosted the *I Dream a World* exhibit, which was attended by record numbers of visitors. The annual Seattle Heritage Award was presented to Esther Mumford, chronicler of local African American history. In 1992, as a continuation of the exhibit, the museum, through sponsorship of US West Foundation which toured the exhibit, began what it hopes will be an annual Summer Intern Program by employing Katherine Mitchell, a Western Washington graduate student in the School of Communications.

One of the museum's volunteers, Al Smith, bought a camera in China in 1929, mastered photography and documented much of Seattle's African American social life for the next fifty years. Smith has received several awards, and was honored for his work in a 1987 retrospective at the

Douglass-Truth Library, sponsored by the **Black Heritage Society of Washington State.** MOHAI presented a sampling of his work in 1986.

From the museum, follow Lake Washington Boulevard, winding eastward and then southward through the Arboreteum until you reach Madison Street. (The #48 bus on Montlake crosses Madison where a transfer to the #11 East Madison may be made.) At the traffic light turn left onto Madison and drive half a block, turning left again at the small commercial plaza at 31st E. to reach Blackbird Books, 3130 E. Madison Street, 325-3793, Monday-Saturday, 10am to 7pm.

Blackbird Books was opened in 1989 by **Joseph Zimbabwe,** a former Los Angeles church pastor and operator of a homeless shelter. This four hundred square foot store has stocked nearly one hundred thousand books since its opening. Here may be found books for children and the general reader on a wide variety of African and African American subjects, cards, original artwork and information about current readings, discussions and booksignings.

When a reception was held at the New Orleans Café for **Charles Johnson** shortly after he received the National Book Award for his novel *Middle*

Joseph Zimbabwe, owner of Blackbird Books.
(Bob Pickens, The People's Photo Studio)

Passage, the author, upon surveying some of the books brought to the occasion from Blackbird Books, chuckled audibly and remarked that he had not seen some of his early titles for years. But such is the resourcefulness of Zimbabwe, who will search for requested titles, out-of print books and limited editions.

From this part of the street it's easy to overlook the **Scoop du Jour Ice Creamery** in Madison Park which was begun by the **Washington** family in 1985. So head eastward to *4029 East Madison,* where you will find "soul" in the peach cobbler ice cream or frozen yogurt, in addition to a multiple offering of other flavors, both plain and fancy. A light lunch may be purchased here as well. Before resuming the tour, catch up on the latest in music at the **Little Record Mart,** *2811 East Madison,* the oldest African American owned record shop in the county. Here you will find "anything that's in print." *Open: Monday-Saturday 11am-8pm, Sunday 12pm-5pm.*

The only public school in the county named for an African American, the **Martin Luther King School,** *3201 East Republican,* is a few blocks southeast of here. **Fern Johnson Proctor** remembers attending the old Harrison School which preceded it, and the neighborhood when her family moved there in 1910: "There were lots of empty lots, and lots of trees. I remember people herding the cows in at milking time. And the pigs would be running around." Martin Luther King School was formerly headed by **Louise McKinney** who created the Early Childhood Model which is used by more than fifty Seattle schools. McKinney's program emphasized early diagnosis of learning problems, analysis of children's strengths, instruction geared to learning rates, and strong parental involvement. The program's motto is "All Children Can Learn." Principal **Betty Gray** and her staff continue McKinney's commitment to educational excellence.

Head westward along Madison and pause to meet Trinidad-Tobago native **Wilson Delancy, Sr.** at Delancy's Afrikan/American Gallery, *2739 East Madison, 322-2863,* and view reasonably-priced art by African, African American and other artists of color. The gallery carries African folk art, prints, posters, African clothing and accessories, and offers framing, dry-mounting and laminating services.

The cards here are unique, many worth framing, and most are unavailable elsewhere in the county. *Hours are 10am-7pm Monday through Thursday, 10am -5pm Friday, 11am-5pm Sunday, closed Saturday.*

Ewajo Center, Inc., *2719 East Madison, 322-0155,* is just across the street at the Madison Plaza. It was founded in 1974 by **Edna Daigre,** a native of Chicago, who has taught dance in Seattle since 1973. Classes are offered in children's ballet, creative rhythm and movement, Afro-Caribbean, Cuban, modern dance, jazz, and isorhythmic conditioning. One-on-one,

*Edna Daigre
instructing a
children's dance
class at her Ewajo
Studio about 1985.
(Courtesy Edna
Daigre)*

personally designed
conditioning and
dance workouts are
available on an
appointment basis.
Periodically such
special cultural expressions as **Capoeira,** the African art of self-defense
which was brought by Africans to Brazil in the 16th century, are taught by
specialists offering classes at Ewajo. Occasional master classes and workshops are taught by professional dancers from national and regional dance
companies. Ghanaian master dancer **Kofi Anang** and his wife, Cecilia,
(329-8876), have taught here, as well as in a variety of educational and stage
settings in the Northwest.

During the 1970s and 1980s most women abandoned the custom of wearing hats as part of the well-dressed look, but African American women
continued this favored form of adornment for attending church, luncheons
and other social events, making it possible for a few milliners to remain in
business, and even encouraging others to enter the business. One such
entrepreneur is **Henrietta Price** whose **Henrietta's Hats/Brimming with
Elegance** shop is located in the *Madison Plaza at 2707 East Madison, open
Monday-Saturday, 10am-5pm.* Custom designed hats as well as wedding
headpieces are features of this shop which also presents fashion shows.

While you're in the neighborhood double back to get a glimpse of the
charming little house at *417 29th Avenue E.* (⋀). Virtually unchanged since
its erection in 1927, it was built by **John Henry "Doc" Hamilton** for his

bride, **Blanche Stewart,** with the income from his popular **"908" Club** which he built on 12th Avenue the previous year.

The **"stairstep"** building, *on the south side of Madison between 26th and 27th,* is the oldest structure in the 1980s' revival of this stretch of the street. Constructed by former insurance broker, Central Area Federal Credit Union and Urban League president, **Luther Carr,** and others, it was the first in a planned series of multiple dwellings. Former plans called for a second group, **"Madison Gate,"** which would have been erected between 24th and 26th Avenues, and distinguished by gateway sculpture on either side of Madison. Before its fruition the project was sold to the builder who erected the complex now standing.

On the south side of the street in the 2300 block are two houses which are quite similar. Built a few years after the turn of the century by the same Swedish carpenter, the westernmost house (∧) was occupied by the builder-owner for a few years before he sold it to **James** and **Marie Roston.** Known in Seattle as "Lieutenant" Roston because of his rise through army ranks during the Spanish-American war, he was discharged in 1903. Upon his return to his home state of Massachusetts, he and a group of community leaders launched an unsuccessful campaign to organize a colony of African Americans to emigrate to the Philippine Islands. Some years later Mr.

The house built by John Henry "Doc" Hamilton in 1927 as it appeared in 1935.

and Mrs. Roston moved to New York where Mr. Roston engaged in real estate in Brooklyn.

They moved to Seattle about 1913, bringing with them furniture, paintings, china and other decorative items which were purchased at the turn of the century for their family home in Warren, Massachusetts. Many of these items graced this house which was still occupied by family members in 1992. The house was a favored gathering place of younger members of the community during the first world war and a community drama group was organized here. Then, as now, Roston found that the most intractable problem encountered by African Americans in King County was the lack of employment.

In the first half of the 20th century, men were concentrated in two occupations: beginning about 1900 as railroad porters and waiters; and after diligent effort on the part of Roston in 1922, as cooks and waiters on steamships. The first successful negotiations were with the Admiral Line whose white workers were on strike at the time of Roston's effort. Eugene Coleman's poignant recollection tells how he was recruited as a waiter: "I was waiting for some of the boys in a pool room on James Street, and a man came in there and said 'I want a hundred niggers, I want a hundred niggers. We're gonna take on the Admiral Line.' And I became one of the hundred niggers."

Barred from all but a limited number of menial jobs and small businesses of their own, their employment on the ships and trains enabled them to purchase modest homes in the Madison District.

Now shuttered, the **Ship Scalers Hall** at *2313 East Madison* was purchased when Local 541, Shipscalers, Drydock and Boatworkers Union moved here in 1955 following sale of their downtown Third Avenue building. The union is ninety percent African American.

At the northwest corner of *23rd Avenue at Madison* stands the **Elizabeth James Apartments** for elderly residents, the first private, non-profit senior housing complex in Seattle. It is named in honor of **Elizabeth and James Gideon,** parents of the late **Russell Gideon.** Russell Gideon operated a pharmacy at the southeast corner of 22nd and Madison from the time of his arrival with his wife, **Lillian,** in 1946 until 1959. He was a founder and coordinator of the **Mardi Gras Festival,** forerunner of the **Black Community Festival,** one of the city's oldest Seafair celebrations.

The **Central Area Business League** preceded the **Central Area Chamber of Commerce,** and Russell Gideon was a founding member as well as a charter member, of the **Central Area Kiwanis Club.** His 1977 appointment as Grand Commander of the Council of the Northern jurisdiction of the **Prince Hall Masons** was the first time in eighty-four years that such an appointment of a mason west of the Mississippi had been made. *Ebony* magazine, a national publication, designated Gideon as one of the nation's **100 Most Influential Black Citizens.** He was born in Nova Scotia, Canada, but served in the United States Army, rising to head the Pharmacy Corps at posts in North Africa and Italy. Lillian Gideon, a native of Boston, served with the Red Cross in London and Paris for two years during World War II, and since then, in a myriad of activities in the Seattle community.

In its 1917 handbook, the **Negro Business Men's League of Seattle** states: "While there is a disposition to prevent us from participating in this promised prosperity wave [of the wartime industries].... In spite of all these obstacles there are many opportunities in and about Seattle awaiting the magic touch of the enterprising colored man, from which, if properly handled, the promoters can reap a golden harvest. Corner grocery stores, quick repair shoe shops, market stalls, truck gardens and heneries in the suburbs, berry farms and small dairies in the country as well as other small enterprises...."

Entrepreneurial activity was seen as the antidote to discrimination in employment. African American businesses began in East Madison after the population of 1890s' settlers in the area expanded enough to support small enterprises. At first it was such freestanding businesses as **Robert** and **Anna Clark's** dairy, **Margaret Cogswell's** restaurant, and beginning about 1916, her store, at *2616 East Madison,* and lodging houses beginning in 1908 with the Woodsons' first building at 1820 24th Avenue. By the late 1910s a strip of commercial enterprises between 19th and 22nd had developed on Madison.

The northeast corner of Madison at 22nd is the site of what was, from 1918 until his death in 1985, **Ed Johnson's** coal and fuel business, the oldest business operated by an African American in Washington State. Johnson, the son of Margaret and James Cogswell, moved to Seattle as a teenager with his family in 1910.

He remembered a very different-looking district when he explored it more than eighty years ago: "Twenty-second Avenue was paved in 1910, the year I came here. Where we lived, they called it the 'Hollow', and it took four horses to pull a ton of coal up the street in a wagon. The sidewalks were four by twelve boards and the rest of it was just clay. You step off the board, why, you're lucky to get back on it. They kept cows, and raised gardens. My mother operated a restaurant at 110 Seneca. Then she came out of there and operated a grocery store at 26th and Madison."

Diagonally across the street, in a building now leveled, were such businesses as **The Copper Kettle Restaurant; Hurd's Bakery;** Geneive Miller's hotel, the **Miller**, a favorite after-church gathering place; the **Anzier Theater**, named after the owners, attorney **Clarence Anderson** and realtor and bondsman **Prentice Frazier;** followed later by other small businesses. Because of the uncertainty of their economic health, Black business have often been characterized as "here today, gone tomorrow."

But this continues to be an area of Black enterprise. Some of the stores, restaurants, and recreation halls, are similar to those of seventy years ago. Others, like **Chester Dorsey's Auto Salon**, could only come about in modern times. From his location at *2227 East Madison* and from mobile units Dorsey and his staff clean and recondition motor vehicles, airplanes and boats, most of which were newfangled notions of the well-to-do when his predecessors launched their businesses in the neighborhood.

DeCharlene Williams, a long-term businesswoman in the area, founded the Central Area Chamber of Commerce. Williams owns the building in which her beauty salon and dress shop are housed. For a brief while in the 1980s she operated a branch of her business in Bellevue. Williams authored *The History of the Central Area* in 1990 and initiated the Life Library Project for teen-age self-discovery. She was the 1992 recipient of the **Black Dollar Days Task Force's** African American Business Owner's Award.

The building on the south side of the 2000 block of Madison was designed by Benjamin McAdoo in the late 1940s. **Dr. Robert H. Joyner** has occupied his office there since its opening.

After several locations, **General's Barbecue,** *2023 C East Madison,* now dispenses its signature item along with southern bred catfish. For those in a quandary, a sample "General Lunch" is offered—ribs, hot link, chicken, and beef—accompanied by baked beans and potato salad. The General's bottled hot or regular sauce is available for sale here. Part of the cost is donated for food and housing for the homeless. Medium sized yam and pecan pies are available for takeout, as are peach cobblers.

Formerly known as the **Harrison Madrona Center,** *2036-1/2 East Madison Street,* in the 1970s was a hive of activity focused on youth training, community service and visual and literary artist support. Organized in 1974 by **Cliff Hooper, Sr., Curtis Barnes, Jr.** and others, it was the umbrella organization for the **United Black Artists Guild,** and operated without public funding.

For many people the church is the African American community. It represents unity, dignity, support, and the people's history, including a time when the church was the one gathering place owned by Black people and impervious to the stresses and assaults on their dignity that a hostile

The Mt. Zion Baptist Church in 1920 and 1992
(1992 Photo by Don Mumford)

society levied. The two oldest churches in the county are located on, or near, Madison.

Founders of **Mt. Zion Baptist Church,** some of whom were members of First Baptist Church, began meeting in homes in 1890, and formally organized in 1894. The Mt. Zion congregation, after meeting in rented space and a smaller church constructed in 1906 on the east side of 11th Avenue between Madison and Spring, purchased this site in 1919. The sturdy red brick church which was constructed in 1920 stood at this site until it was razed in 1975 for the erection of the present structure. It was the earliest work of the county's first Black architect, **Harry James,** who moved to Seattle from New Zealand with his family in 1917. Frustrated by the lack of patronage and the small economic base of the local community, he moved to Brazil in the 1920s. Pastored by the Rev. Dr. **Samuel B. McKinney,** Mt. Zion, the largest African American congregation in the state, reflects a broad cross-section of the community. The church's choirs are outstanding. The sanctuary choir, directed and accompanied by **Frank and Phyllis Byrdwell,** is known for its rich repertoire of spirituals, hymns and anthems sung during regular worship services as well as in concert for other churches and performing arts organizations in the Puget Sound region.

The **Mount Zion Ethnic School** was begun by the church in 1979 to promote excellence in education. It meets on Saturdays and is open to any youth between six and sixteen years of age. Young people between sixteen and eighteen are encouraged to participate in teacher assistant training. The school offers courses in African American history, the arts, tutoring, computer education, career exploration and enhancement of self-esteem. The church sponsors an annual art exhibition each spring.

This imposing church of African-inspired design is a landmark in this part of the city. The stained glass windows of the chapel bear images of significant African American historical figures. Artists **Curtis** and **Royal Alley Barnes** rendered the hanging banner in the sanctuary which signifies baptism.

One block up, on the same side of the street, is the Hearing, Speech and Deafness Center, *1620 18th Avenue*, with a renovated exterior which completely conceals the much more graceful structure which served as the Elks clubhouse from the time they purchased it in 1921 until the Great Depression. The original building, surrounded on three sides by a porch with turned posts, was a source of pride for the community. It was one of many

The Elks home in 1927 and 1992 after substantial exterior alteration.
(Who's Who? Among the Colored People of Washington State,
and Bob Pickens, the People's Photo Studio)

buildings lost by members of the African American community during the Depression.

At the opposite end of the block, is the **Ponderosa,** *1602 18th Avenue,* residence of senior citizens which was constructed in 1970 by Russell Gideon, who sold it in 1978.

Continuing westward along Madison, the building at *1500 East Madison,* is the former site of **Eddie Cotton's Famous Soul Burger,** a restaurant owned and operated by the late boxer, who died in 1989, and his friends. In the next block west you will find the oldest African American church in the county, **First African Methodist Episcopal Church,** which

The First African Methodist Episcopal Church is the oldest African American Institution in King County. (David Lee Meyers, 1976)

evolved from a Sunday School that first met in 1886, and since 1890 has occupied the same site with the addition of neighboring lots. Such was the pride of the African American community in this initiative that its founding committee included Episcopalians and Baptists as well as Methodists. The present church building was begun in 1912, with the north wing added in 1989.

When it was nominated to the Seattle Landmarks Register in 1983, this building became the first African American structure in the state to be placed on a register of historic places, fitting recognition of a church which is one of the oldest African American institutions in America, the first having been established in Philadelphia in 1787. Although the beautiful hand-carved walnut pews, purchased with the hard-earned dimes and quarters of early members, were sold in 1983, inscriptions on the stained glass windows which date to the erection of the present church building, evoke a sense of the past. Descendants of some of the founding members still attend the church, while some of the outreach programs, such as tutoring, embrace some of the county's newest residents, Eritrean refugees from the Horn of Africa. Descendants of **John T.** and **Magnolia Scott Gayton** established the church's library in 1989. The church is home to the **FAME Choir**, a fine group of young a capella singers who continue the tradition of spirituals, while including contemporary renditions in their performances. A strong tutoring and mentoring program under the direction of **Frances Carr** is one of the unsung contributions to the community. The church, pastored by the Rev. David Oxley, owns the Imperial Apartments, *1427 East Pike Street*, which are occupied by low-income families.

Many of the titles relating to Africans and African Americans at Pathfinder Bookstore, *1405 East Madison*, are unavailable elsewhere in the county. Their postcard selection is also unique.

Madison and First Hill, Route 2
Head south across the Mountlake Bridge, traveling along Mountlake Boulevard then 24th Avenue to 23rd Avenue, to explore an alternative route when leaving the University District.

On the east side of the street is a small business building where **James** and **Harriet Salisbury** operated a photography studio, *1000 Turner Way E.*, (just where 24th Avenue bends is Turner Way) producing high quality photographs. James Salisbury, a graduate of Brooks School of Photography in California, has had prints in circulation worldwide in the loan collection of the International Exhibit of Professional Photographers.

Salisbury photographed many of Seattle's most notable citizens and documented community events during the 1970s.

During that decade an overgrown gully at *24th and East Harrison* in the back of Prentice and Clara Frazier's home was developed into a mini-park which was called Harrison Park. In 1983, with the support of hundreds of community residents, **Otis Bean,** nephew of Prentice Frazier, succeeded in having the name of this park changed to Frazier in honor of one of the community's most active citizens during the first half of the twentieth century. Prentice Ivanhoe Frazier, a former bank partner in Texas prior to moving to Seattle in 1916, operated several businesses here ranging from undertaking to newspaper publishing to bail bondsman. He was a staunch member of the First African Methodist Church, and an avid supporter of children and their welfare. The Frazier home is at *410 23rd Avenue East* (∧).

For a brief while the house at *424 24th Avenue E.* (∧) was the realization of a dream of the University of Washington **Black Student Union** to establish a day-care and cultural center for Central Area children in 1971. The effort was led by twin sisters **Wanda** and **Tyra Hackett,** Gonzaga University BSU charter members before they transferred to the UW. Their diligence included six months of fund-raising and taking night classes in order to staff the center during the day, while holding part-time jobs. This modest dream house was called "**Mahalikwa Watoto,**" Swahili for "a children's place."

In addition to the African American homes and buildings designed and constructed by carpenters or master builders, some of the structures were designed by the occupants.

When **Ernest Attucks White** was mustered out of the army in 1918, he decided to move to Seattle rather than return to Spokane. After he married **Essie Jones** they looked for a house, encountering discrimination in practically every neighborhood in Seattle. They purchased a lot on which the house that Mr. White designed still stands at *2404 E. Thomas Street* (∧), and spent the rest of their lives there. Mrs. White preceded Mr. White in death. A mail carrier for thirty-nine and a half years, he died in 1978.

The Adelphi Apartment block, *230 23rd Avenue E. at Thomas,* which was purchased by a group of African American businessmen in 1923, and continues to provide reasonably-priced housing to a number of tenants of various races, is a monument to Black entrepreneurship of the 1920s. It was purchased at a time when informal covenants restricted selling properties north of Madison to African Americans. Shortly after this purchase, formal written covenants came into common usage in most parts of the city.

In this neighborhood are four apartment complexes of seven which were designed and built by the firm of Peck and Merriwether in 1969. Howard University graduate C. Raymond Merriwether was a partner in this firm which, under the Federal Housing Administration's program for non-profit sponsored housing, purchased the land, designed, and built these buildings which house about six hundred and fifty people. The buildings are named after famous African Americans from other parts of the country: **The Dunbar**, *2200 East John Street*, named after the early 20th century poet, novelist and playwright Paul Laurence Dunbar; **Bethune Manor**, *2200 East Republican Street*, named after Florida college founder, women's advocate, and teacher Mary McCleod Bethune; **Langston House**, *19th and East Republican Street*, named after poet, novelist and playwright, Langston Hughes; **The Charles Drew**, named for the blood plasma pioneer. A fifth building, the **Catalina Apartments**, is located at *111 25th Avenue E.*

The building at *102 21st Avenue E.*, with exterior modifications, housed the Phyllis Wheatley Branch YWCA from the early 1920s through the 1930s.

Marcella Fusilier's Seattle Doll Hospital, *222 19th Avenue E.* (/^), was at this house for many years. Broken, bruised, loved-to-death dolls were made like new by this self-taught expert. Dolls from as far away as Canada were brought or sent to this house for mending.

Architect **Benjamin McAdoo** designed the four-plex at *401-409 19th Avenue E.*, for Gerald and Elizabeth Wells in the 1953. The homeowners lived in one of the apartments and rented the others. In 1911, Gerald Wells was considered one of the finest jazz flutists in the world. A native ofGrenada, West Indies, he came to California about 1919 and moved to Seattle in 1928. Gerald Wells was president of the **African American Musician's Union**, Local #493 during the 1930s. His late wife, Elizabeth Wells, remembered those days in a 1976 interview: "The Musicians' Union office was in our home, in our hallway, really. You'd have to pay each year for the charter, and of course, none of them had any money, including my husband, and so I'd have to get the charter for them. Women were able to find jobs more (readily) than men."

Elizabeth Wells was brought to Seattle from Galveston, Texas, in 1918, by her family, when she was nine years old. She attended school in Ballard and helped to found the Central Area Federal Credit Union. In the early 1970s, Ms. Wells received first prize in the Washington Credit Union

League Publication Contest for her monthly *Briefs* which she published
on credit union matters.

*Head south on 19th Avenue turning right at Madison Street, and remain
on it until you reach Broadway. Turn left onto Broadway.*

Stop by the **La Mediterranean Delicatessen,** *528 Broadway, 329-8818,*
and choose some of **Jocelyn Owens'** delicious sauces. The flavors include
Spicy Peanut, Creole Jambalaya, and Cajun Come Back Sauces. Owens
was designated an official Goodwill Games Caterer in 1990. She was reputed to be the first person in Washington to have bottled a hot sauce for
sale. Owens also features boudin blanc, a white sausage, prepared from
an old family recipe.

Raymond Merriwether encouraged the First Baptist Church to con-
struct Hilltop House, the eleven-story building at *1005 Terry Street at Terrace,* for senior citizens of moderate income. Following a meeting with
church leaders, he and another member were asked to explore site possi-
bilities, and at Merriwether's suggestion, the present site was purchased
and built upon in 1969 with assistance from the federal government.
Merriwether drew up the preliminary loan application and served as loan
consultant for research and preparation of the application.

One of the first residents of the building was **Bertha Pitts Campbell,** a
founder of the international **Delta Sigma Theta Sorority** at Howard University in Washington, D.C. in 1913. Ms. Campbell lived in the building
until her death in 1990, two months before her 101st birthday.

Bertha Campbell, her husband Earl, and her son Earl, Jr., moved to
Seattle from Grand Junction, Colorado in 1923. In the ensuing years, she
helped establish a local chapter of the sorority and was active in the
YWCA, for which she volunteered for forty years.

As board representative to the Seattle YWCA, Ms. Campbell attended
several meetings where racial restrictions prevented her from voting before
she gently, but firmly, informed the board that as a duly elected
representative of her branch of the Young Women's *Christian* Association,
she would have to have the same right to vote as as any other board
member, to which the startled white board members acquiesced, making
her the first African American woman in the United States to have such a
vote. This assertiveness and advocacy for full participation of African
Americans, and later, the elderly, in American life was a hallmark of this
quiet woman who graduated valedictorian of her 1908 class at Montrose
(Colorado) High School. During her ninety-eighth year she spearheaded

a campaign against erection of the parking garage to the east of her building because of the threatened loss of view and gardening space of the tenants.

Her sorority sponsors an annual **Bertha Pitts Campbell Fun Run** each spring. In 1981, Wing Luke Elementary School principal **Pauline Hill** and **Sherilyn Jordan** wrote *Too Young to be Old,* (Peanut Butter Publishing) a biography of her life.

A few blocks north, *505 Ninth Avenue*, is the building that for many years was the office of **Dr. Walter Scott Brown** who, in 1948, opened the first outpatient clinic for plastic and reconstructive surgery in the nation.

CENTRAL AREA

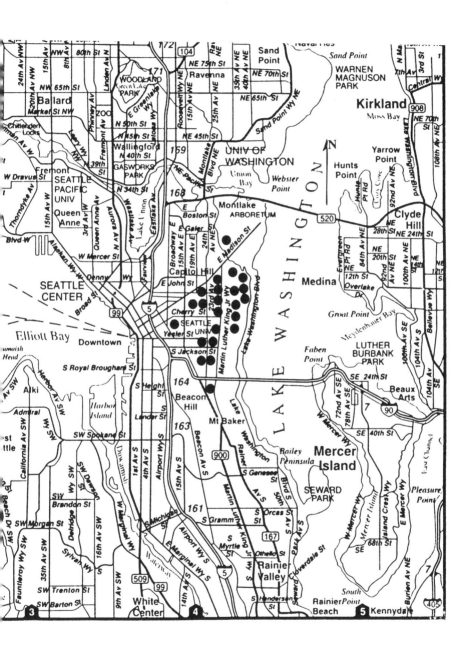

8.
Central Area

Legacy of the Pioneers
Vestiges of the oldest Africn American neighborhood in the county may be
seen by traveling along 23rd Avenue (bus #48) and neighboring streets.

The first African American family, **Seaborn J. Collins** and his wife, **Alzada**,
moved to East Madison when they built their home on 27th Avenue, just
north of Madison, in 1888. But the nucleus of the 19th century settlement
is two blocks south of Madison and east of 23rd Avenue.

In the 1980s, with the increase in housing costs in the area, the African
American population declined in some areas as much as twenty-six percent,
with a similar decline in home ownership.

The **AME Zion Church** was founded in New York in 1796. The predecessor of **Ebenezer African Methodist Episcopal Zion Church,** *1716 23rd*
Avenue, 322-6620, was **Kyles Temple,** which stood at Sixth Avenue and
Main Street, until construction of the Yesler Terrace Housing Project required razing or removal of the structures between Fifth and Twelfth Avenues, Main Street and Yesler Way in 1939. The Kyles church building was
bought by the budding **Goodwill Baptist Church** congregation which was
headed by the late **Rev. Norman Mitchell.**

West Indian emigrants figured prominently in the establishment of the
present AMEZ church. The **Rev. Henry Leon Johnston,** formerly a Jamaican carriage maker, who was assigned to the congregation in 1926, was
joined in the effort to build the present structure by such friends of his as
Archie Tudor, a Barbadian ship carpenter and realtor who came to Seattle in 1929, and Jamaican **Edward Pitter,** a former Episcopalian who
arrived in 1909. They were joined in the effort by **George Moore,** a
Tacoman who became **Booker T. Washington's** secretary in the late 1910s
and **Peter DeBow,** editor of the Seattle *Searchlight* which he began in 1903.
In 1927 Pitter and DeBow published *Who's Who? Among the Colored*
People of Washington State.

Ebenezer was organized in the home of **Edward and Majorie Allen Pitter.**
Their three daughters, **Maxine, Constance** and **Marjorie,** recruited children for the Sunday School by enticing them with home-baked cookies. So
successful were their efforts that, until the church building was built, it
became necessary to rent **Chandler's Hall,** a meeting space owned by the

late turn-of-the-century arrival, **William Chandler** and his family who owned a fuel business for many years. The hall stood just west of the northwest corner of 23rd Avenue and Madison Street until 1980.

Unlike earlier churches, the incorporation papers of 1933 include the names of two women: **Marjorie Pitter** and **Sarah E. Dawson.** Tacoman **Eddie Smith** drew the blue prints for the church shortly after his graduation from the University of Washington. The plans, which included a brick exterior and a parsonage to the rear, were scaled down with the continuation of the Great Depression.

The bulk of the construction was performed by **Pastor Johnston, Harry Ellis,** and **J. Taylor,** but many parishoners, including the young Pitter sisters, actually sawed wood and drove nails to erect the church.

In 1930 the church bought three houses that occupied the site of the power station at 22nd and 23rd Avenues between Pike and Pine, and relocated them. During the depression WPA sewing classes were held in the basement of one of the houses, a duplex in the 100 block of 22nd Avenue. Church services were held there on Sundays until the construction of the present building.

Like Mt. Zion at an earlier time, Ebenezer had a marching band in the 1930s and a drill team. They marched in the old Potlatch parades, precursor to Seafair, and the church entered floats.

Ebenezer played an important role during World War II in welcoming newly-arrived wartime workers and servicemen to Seattle. With the help

Ebenezer AME Zion Church was founded in this house owned by the Pitter family.
(Don Mumford, 1992)

of the War Commission, the church basement was completed with bath facilities and sleeping accomodations. Military personnel visiting the local U.S.O. at the YMCA next door had only to walk a few yards for hostel accomodations. Some of the military families became active members of the church. The church held services at the chapel at Camp George Jordan (*Fourth Avenue S. and Spokane*) where African American soldiers were stationed, and at Fort Lawton in the afternoon of each first Sunday of the month. It continues its outreach services with a food bank.

In the fall of 1991, the church suffered extensive interior damage from firebombs. With an outpouring of interracial, interdenominational support the church was rededicated in the spring of 1992. There are two congregations of this denomination in King County, the second being **Catherine AMEZ** in the Rainier Valley. Ebenezer is pastored by the Rev. L. J. Thompson.

The **East Madison Y.M.C.A.**, *1700 23rd Avenue, 322-6969*, was established in the early l940s. The building, **Leon Bridges'** first job as a licensed architect, was dedicated in 1965. It is on part of the original twelve acres purchased by William and Sarah Grose in 1882. This is the former site of the **Alpha Tennis and Outing Club** which was formed by area residents in 1915. The club hosted weddings, receptions, meetings, and dances as well as tennis. Tournaments were held at the tennis courts at 23rd and Cherry. The "Y" provides a variety of services to the neighborhood, including swimming and summer day camp and a **Young Achievers** program which seeks to raise academic standards of inner city youth while exposing them to diverse career options and providing successful role models.

Rounding the corner at Olive onto 24th Avenue, where Howell Street ends, note the farmhouse at *1733 24th Avenue*. It is the former home of **William** and **Sarah Grose** (∧), built by the Groses after the Seattle Fire of 1889 reduced their waterfront "Our House" hotel to ashes. In 1876 the Groses purchased four lots at Fifth Avenue and James on which they built rental houses. The East Madison land was purchased for one thousand dollars in gold and used as a ranch operated by hired hands. In the 1890s this house was second in importance only to the African Methodist Church as a gathering place for the county's small African American middle class.

Capt. W. D. Matthews, one of the country's small number of commissioned African American officers during the Civil War was a guest here, as were other distinguished national figures. In a 1936 letter to the Groses' grandson **William Dixon,** their daughter, **Lizzie Oxendine,** remembered their early years in East Madison: "...Madison was the only street that was graded. There was nothing but roads and trails through fallen trees, stumps and underbrush. No street lights. When we went to church at night we carried our lanterns....The old homestead was not on any street but stood in the orchard at this time. The twelve acres was intact. There was no street running through at all." Three generations of Grose family members grew up here.

Some of the Groses' original furniture is now in the New Jersey home of **Carrolle Fair Perry**, great, great granddaughter of William and Sarah Grose. A mini-park named after William Grose is located on 30th Avenue between Denny and Howell. The park was developed after strenuous effort by the Madison Valley Concerned Citizens, and dedicated in 1983 with the name proposed by the **Black Heritage Society of Washington State.** *(P.O. Box 22961, Seattle 98122-0961)*

The Seattle *Republican* newspaper remarked in 1908 that, "on the property may be found a most choice variety of fruit trees, flowers and all such things that go to bless and beautify a home." Remnants of the old family orchard remained on the lot just south of the house until the construction of the condominium building in 1985.

The residence at *1735 24th Avenue* (∧), on the north side of the Grose home, was built by the Groses' granddaughter **Carrie Dixon** and her husband, postal clerk William Black, in the late 1910s. Grose descendants lived in both of these houses until the mid-1970s. Over the years lots in the Grose tract were sold, often to African Americans, giving rise to the development of an area referred to by 1890s journalists as a "colored colony" or, in the more derogatory fashion of the day, "coons' hollow."

The former residence of the **John F. Cragwell** family is at *1712 24th Avenue* (∧). Cragwell's well-furnished barbershops in such downtown hotels as the Butler, the Seattle, and the New Washington earned him notice in a 1923 *Sunset* magazine article and other periodicals earlier in the century. He accompanied the U.S. Post Master General to Seattle in 1890 and moved with his family to Seattle from Washington, D.C. a year later. During his forty-year operation, Cragwell sometimes employed as many as eighteen barbers at the same time in his shops. He was appointed by the governor to the State Barber's Commission in 1901.

The building known as the **Cascade View Apartments,** *1820 24th Avenue*, was formerly known as The Woodson. By the end of World War I every house except one on the 1800 block of 24th Avenue was occupied by an African American family. **Zacharias** and **Irene Patterson Woodson** and their two sons were among the first families to purchase nearby property. The Woodsons built the apartment house in 1908, in anticipation of the expected need for housing during Seattle's first world's fair, the Alaska-Yukon-Pacific Exposition of 1909. They proudly offered electric lights and porcelain bath tubs to adjoining apartments and furnished a telephone, all for seventeen dollars and fifteen cents a month. A couple of years later,

The Woodson Apartments before and after exterior modification. Upper photograph with original owners, Irene and Zacharias Woodson, on upper balcony, taken about 1909. Lower photo taken in 1992. (Don Mumford)

they built a second apartment building on the lot to the north of the present building, which has since been demolished. The Woodsons arrived in Seattle in 1897 and were in the apartment and rooming house business until the 1930s. This building has undergone exterior modification.

In 1917 **Corrine Carter**, wife of the Rev. **W. D. Carter**, pastor of Mt. Zion Baptist Church, organized the **Phyllis Wheatley Branch YWCA**, named after the African-born Revolutionary War era poet. It offered living accommodations to women and girls, meeting rooms, classes in millinery, dressmaking, and "charm," as well as an employment bureau. A Children's Orthopedic Hospital guild is named for Mrs. Carter in recognition of her efforts in establishing the "Y."

The first home of the organization was at this house, *1807 24th Avenue* (∿), long since returned to its original usage as a private residence. Its first occupants after its return to a private dwelling were Rilla Varlack and her husband, William P., who moved to Seattle from San Francisco in 1914. "Madame Varlack" was well-known in the early part of the century for her skin and hair preparations. Her niece, **Rilla Allen,** who came from Chicago to live with them in 1923, remembered: "Much of what she used in her salon was based on her own formulas, and it seemed to be good. She didn't write them down, or I've never seen a list of ingredients or anything. I wish now that I had asked her. I don't know what she used. I really wasn't paying much attention in those days."

Edward and Marjorie Pitter bought the fifteen room house at *1532 24th Avenue* (∿), with servants' quarters in the basement, in the 1920s. The family often shared their home with newcomers to Seattle and others in need of transitional housing. They were very active in the social and political life of the African American population. The Ebenezer AMEZ Church was organized at this house in 1926. Ed Pitter served as King County deputy sheriff and deputy clerk prior to his retirement as a county employee in 1964.

Marjorie Pitter was a dedicated civil rights campaigner, who worked diligently for the abolition of discrimination in the work-place during World War II. A scholarship bearing her name and that of her husband, Edward, is offered annually by the Lutheran Church of the Good Shepherd which they joined in the early 1940s. The Pitters' daughters are the subject of **"The Academic and Extracurricular Undergraduate Experiences of Three Black Women at the University of Washington, 1935-1941,"**

Juana Royster's doctoral dissertation, which was written in 1981 for her Ph.D. degree from the University of Washington.

Constance Pitter Thomas, who completed a degree in education, was barred from teaching by rigid hiring segregation in Seattle before World War II.

Maxine Haynes, who had been discouraged by UW Nursing faculty from pursuing a nursing degree, graduated with a degree in sociology, and pursued nursing out of state. When African American students demanded African American faculty at the UW, she was recruited to teach in the School of Nursing. **Marjorie King** was appointed to serve one term in the legislature in 1964-65.

The **Royal Vista Apartments** (formerly the Douglas Apartments), *114 24th Avenue E.*, were built a few years prior to The Woodson. The complex has been occupied primarily by African Americans since its purchase by a group of businessmen headed by former New Zealand contractor, E. R. James, in 1917.

The **Augustus** and Edith Bown family was living here at the time of the 1929 Wall Street Crash when **Mrs. Edith Ruth Cahill Bown** withdrew the family's last five hundred dollars from the bank to purchase a piano, a decision which bewildered her family throughout the dismal years of the Depression. Although resources were stretched to the limit, the Bown children were given music and dance lessons. Two of the daughters, **Edith Mary Bown Valentine** and **Patti Bown**, became renowned pianists. As a high school student in the 1940s Patti played at the governor's mansion with the Seattle Symphony Orchestra. She was offered forty-seven music scholarships when she graduated from Immaculate Conception High School in 1949.

Patti Bown studied classical European music at Seattle University, the University of Washington and Cornish School of the Arts to please her mother. But jazz was her first love. In time she was musical director for Sarah Vaughn and Dinah Washington. Her compositions have been recorded by Duke Ellington, Count Basie and Seattleite Quincy Jones. Edith Mary Valentine made her professional debut at New York's Carnegie Hall in the 1950s.

Edith Ruth Bown, theirr mother, a **Fisk University** graduate, later founded the St. Peter Claver Society, an outreach mission of Catholic African Americans, in her home at *118 22nd Avenue E.*, in the 1930s. Sisters Millie and Augustine live in Seattle. Augustine Bown Walker, who also studied music, works for the Seattle Housing Authority. Dr. Millie Bown Russell, biology lecturer, and assistant to the vice president in the Office of Minority Affairs at the University of Washington, was a founding member of the Black Friends of Yesler Library, and is a member of **Alpha Kappa Alpha Sorority** which began the library's African-American Collection, and the **Seattle-Mombasa** (Kenya) and **Seattle-Limbe** (Cameroon) **Sister City Associations.** These associations organized a successful effort in 1987 to send donated medical aid vans, medical supplies and books to the sister cities. In 1992 several members of the associations began a long-range effort to aid African countries under duress. Somalia was the focus of this assistance in 1992.

The **City of Seattle's Office of International Affairs,** *700 Third Avenue, Suite 440, Seattle 98104-1809; telephone 684-8055,* publishes a newsletter four times a year, often with information on sister cities.

In the days when East Madison seemed a long way from Downtown, small farms and gardens flourished here, and practically every family kept a cow and a horse at the back of the house. **Robert** and **Anna Clark** and their children operated a small dairy at *111 25th Avenue E.,* from 1890 to 1895 when Robert Clark went into the transfer business. The Clarks were founding members of the Mt. Zion Baptist Church and early employers of African American women.

Until the death of **Beatrice Chatters** in 1990, her family home at *206 25th Avenue E.,* was synonymous with the Chatters home and hand laundry, which the family operated in the early years of the twentieth century. Ms. Chatters perished in the fire which destroyed the home. The laundry, which stood at the northeast corner of the intersection with John Street, was demolished some years earlier.

Plum Tree Park, *west side 26th Avenue between Olive and Howell,* is one of dozens of tiny parks found throughout Seattle, and one of several in the area with an African American association. In 1982 Seattle Parks and Recreation Department established its "Adopt-A-Park" Program to involve residents of the city in the care and maintenance of parks. The first volunteer in the city was **Tyree Scott,** a neighborhood resident who assumed the task of regular litter control and basic gardening maintenance of this handkerchief-sized park. Scott was jailed several times for leading construction workers in closures of sites that discriminated against African American workers during the 1960s and 1970s. In recent years he and his family have lived, and worked on development projects, in Mozambique.

The **Washington Home and Studio,** *1816 26th Avenue,* qualified for designation as a historic landmark because of its association with the life of a contributor to the city's cultural heritage. The entire site—the interior and exterior of the house, studio and yard—of sculptor **James Washington, Jr.,** was added to the Seattle Register of Historic Landmarks in March of

1991, only the second such designation of an African American-related property in the city. (The First African Methodist Church is the other.)

Like thousands of African Americans James and Janie Rogella Washington came to Seattle for employment during World War II. They are the second owners of this craftsman bungalow which has had very little alteration, except exterior siding, since it was built in 1918. This type of house was built in large numbers throughout Seattle after the turn of the century. The Washingtons purchased theirs in 1948, about the time that James Washington began to paint while still working in the Bremerton Naval ship yard as an electrician. During a trip to Mexico in 1950 he was inspired to switch from painting to sculpting, and it is with the latter that he is most closely identified. Although he studied briefly with painter Mark Tobey in the late 1940s, he is primarily self -taught.

For three days during the fall of 1966, visitors came and went during the opening celebration of the sculptor's studio, a two-story, split level structure at the back of the residence which was designed by William Bayne. Japan's famed sculptor, Isamu Noguchi and his assistant, visited Washington there on his visit to Seattle in preparation for "Black Sun" at the Capitol Hill grounds of the Seattle Art Museum. Washington collaborated on some of the specific work areas of the studio. A recipient of numerous awards and recognitions, he is one of one hundred Washingtonians included in the 1989 *"Washington Centennial Hall of Honor"* exhibition and book. Washington is the subject of *The Spirit in the Stone, the Visionary Art of James W. Washington, Jr.* by Dr. Paul J. Karlstrom.

James Booker, a partner of Charles Harvey in the Handicap Company, which burned down with the city in 1889, built the house at the end of the block at *1837 26th Avenue* (∿), in 1905. The house's interior and exterior are virtually unchanged since its construction.

It is a seven-block walk from 26th Avenue to the next two sites. For a shorter walk the #2 East Union bus may be taken.

The Browning-Tom Green House, *2919 East Howell Street* (∿), was the first house design executed by Benjamin McAdoo after he began his independent practice in 1947. The commission by the first owners, Dr. James P. and Mrs. Ola Browning allowed him free rein of his talent, and it brought McAdoo enough income to allow him to buy his first office space which was constructed in the basement of the duplex across the street *2920 East Howell Street* (∿).

A native of Pasadena, California, McAdoo received his architecture degree from the University of Washington in 1946. He was inspired by Paul Revere Williams, the great, but largely unknown African American architect of Los Angeles, to whom he had been introduced as a teenager. McAdoo designed numerous homes in the Puget Sound, several of which received the American Institute of Architects "Home of the Month" award. One of the homes was selected as "Home of the Year" in 1957. About twenty Seventh Day Adventist churches in the Northwest were designed by McAdoo, as were several banks, apartment houses, businesses and buildings in city and county recreation areas.

In the early part of the 20th century **William Presto,** an 1890s Cuban immigrant, sold lots in the area east of Martin Luther King Way between Denny and Union, further extending African American settlement beyond the Grose Purchase. The house at *3001 East Denny Way* (∧), is still referred to by senior members of the African American community as **The Presto House.**

Union-Cherry Sampler
Follow Denny east to 34th Avenue and proceed southward. If traveling by bus, the #2 East Union may be taken to 34th and Union, two blocks south of the next site.

Al Larkins Park, *northeast corner of 34th and Pike,* was dedicated in 1986 to honor Larkins who came to Seattle in 1943. He arrived as part of the **Jive Bombers,** a group of professional jazz musicians at the Sandpoint Naval Base, whose prowess and anonymity approach that of accomplished players of the old Negro Baseball League.

Alvin William Larkins, born in Baltimore, was a social worker and teacher. Raised as an Episcopalian, he served as choir director at Madrona Presbyterian Church for many years. He was the first African American in the 1963 Seattle World's Fair Marching Band, and a member of the Rainy City Jazz Band. Upon his death in 1977 the Al Larkins Memorial Fund of Franklin High School was established for African American students seeking a college education.

The Carolyn Downs Community Clinic, *1422 34th Avenue,* is a lasting legacy of the **Black Panther Party** which established this clinic after the party's founding in 1968. Originally called the **Sidney Miller Free Medical Clinic,** it was the realization of the party's goal to provide and improve access to health and social services for Central Area African Americans. It presently bears the name of a deceased early member who helped to establish the party's medical program, and continues the ideal of providing medical care for all persons regardless of ability to pay. An Eddie Walker mural painted in 1977 is in the reception area of the clinic.

Greater Friendship Missionary Baptist Church (formerly Black Arts West Theater), *3406 East Union Street,* was the performing arts center and gallery of one of the most talked-about African American theaters in the nation during the 1970s. The theater's organization began at a time when African American participation in the arts was just becoming visible. Lorna Richards in her introduction to the 1979 *Directory of Black Artists and Arts Resources (Arts Resource Service)* states, "To number the Black artists in the Seattle area at something less than a hundred would have been generous in 1972…two hundred [artists] are listed in this directory. The final number could easily have been higher." Interest in the arts was gradually rekindled in the late 1960s, giving rise to two theater groups, the **Soul Search Players** and the **New Group Theatre.** Prior to the formation of **Black Arts/West,** a Model Cities project which was formed in 1969 from a merger of the two groups, **Lorraine Hansberry's** *Raisin in the Sun* played here in the summer of 1961 at what was then Gene Keene's Cirque Theatre. The cast included **Doug Barnett,** who later formed the New Group Theatre; **Roberta Byrd Barr,** the first African American principal of a Seattle high school, as well as **Greg Morris,** at that time a recent University of Iowa graduate who wore a turban and livery as a waiter in the old Golden Lion restaurant at the Olympic Hotel. At the end of the season he headed down to California where a few years later he obtained a leading role in the long-running television program "Mission Impossible."

A variety of natural foods from various places in the world, and some of fabric artist and ceramicist **Monad's** artwork may be purchased at **Pure Manifestation,** located at *1135 34th Avenue, 322-4822.* Beautiful, hand-constructed drums by the artist are also on display and for sale. His whistle sculptures never fail to surprise. In 1991 he received one of five "Arts Against Racism" grants from the King County Arts Commission for a large bronze whistle which is underway. Monad has taught children's classes at the Pacific Arts Center at Seattle Center and presented programs at the Seattle Public Library.

Whether your preference runs to a cowboy hat with unique finishing, or a Sunday go-to-meeting hat, the **Alice M. Conley Hat Manufacturing Company,** *1112 34th Avenue, 322-1868,* is one of very few in the county where it can be custom-made by a skilled local craftsman. This small company is named in honor of the mother of the owner, **Alexander Conley.**

It's worth a visit just to see this tradition carried on. *Open Monday-Saturday, 11am-6pm.*

The **Madrona Playfield,** *34th and Marion,* as well as the **Garfield** *(26th and Cherry)* and **Leschi** *(now Powell Barnett Park)* fields were developed by the Central Area Motivation Programs' Department of Beautification, which also made improvements at Colman Playfield. Headed by **Garcia Massingale** and his assistant, **Frank Waynewood,** the beautification department, begun in 1965 with Office of Economic Opportunity funds, pursued a two-fold purpose: 1) to involve the entire Central Area in a self-improvement beautification project and 2) to employ and provide skills to people labelled as the "hard-core unemployable." As part of the playground construction and installation projects, workers were taught basic carpentry, concrete mixing and pouring, plumbing, gardening, landscaping, soil values and methods of planting, caring for and pruning trees and shrubs. Social skills and on-the-job counseling were provided by department administrators and volunteer psychiatrists, social workers, businessmen, law enforcement representatives and financial consultants.

About twenty-five hundred maples were planted throughout the area by CAMP's beautification department. A letter from the city arborist, Marvin E. Black, to the *FACTS* newspaper in 1983 stated, in part: "...I want to compliment the Central Area for how well they respect the trees on their streets. The Central Area has the lowest vandalism of the street trees of all the parts of Seattle.... This is a powerful tribute to the community's parents and leaders who have taught their youth not to destroy but to value beauty and life."

Most of the trees along parking strips of the Central Area today date from CAMP's innovative, well-financed program of the 1960s and early 1970s. The trees at the sitting park north of the **Medgar Evers Pool,** *on 23rd Avenue,* partially funded by the Park Department, were also part of this project.

Fr. O. J. McGowan, of the Campus Ministries at Seattle University and pastor of St. Therese Church, *3416 East Marion Street, 325-2711,* was, upon his ordination, the first African American priest in Washington. The **first Pan African Mass of Peace and Goodwill,** held at St. James Cathedral during the Goodwill Games of 1990, was directed by Fr. McGowan. St. Therese's delightful "Shades of Praise" choir and Immaculate Conception's gospel choir, directed by talented pianist and composer, **Kent Stevenson,** and joined by others, sang for this mass. Former Pacific Northwest Ballet

School faculty member and dancer **Kabby Mitchell** was lead dancer and choreographer.

The storefront at *1127-1/2 34th Avenue,* was the former office of the Seattle Black Panther Party, which, at the time of its organization in April of 1968, was the second branch of the party established in the United States. The party coordinated voter registration, sicle cell anemia screening, prison visitations, clothing and food banks, fielded at least one candidate for political office, and operated a long-term free breakfast program for children which at one time was offered at five different sites. Brothers **Elmer** and **Aaron Dixon,** two of the founding members of this remarkable group of young people, are writing a book on the party. *Hands Off Aaron Dixon,* a booklet published by the Aaron Dixon Defense Fund in 1968 contains a history of the organization and two poems by Aaron Dixon, who won prizes in poetry and had some of his poems published in the 1960s.

The **Madrona Community Center,** (Madrona Presbyterian Church), *832 32nd Avenue,* has served the arts and the surrounding community since the 1970s. It was the first home of Steve Sneed's **Madrona Youth Theater,** and offered discussions and workshops on pertinent issues. In 1979 Sam Pierce painted a Black History Mural which is in the main meeting room.

Fire Chief **Claude Harris** was assigned to Old Fire Station #12 (now Sally Goldmark Branch library), *33rd Avenue and Union Street,* as a rookie in 1959, and appointed Seattle Fire Chief in 1985. He is chairman of the seventy thousand member Metropolitan Fire Chiefs' Section of the International Association of Fire Chiefs from the United States, Canada, Europe and Australia.

You may end the tour here, or continue your exploration of the Central Area. Bus #2 East Union stops across the street from the library.

The leisurely-paced, busy shop known as **Sam's Super Burgers,** *2600 East Union Street. (329-4870)* was opened in 1982 after Sammie Phillips moved from her Yesler Way restaurant after eleven years. Everything here comes in a bun. The emphasis is on hamburgers, although it is possible to order variants of hot dogs, as well. Local African American newspapers are available while you wait, as are umbrella-covered tables on the outside.

Emerald City Bank, (formerly Liberty Bank), *2320 East Union Street,* was founded by a group of Central Area residents in 1968. It is the only African American bank in the state.

At **Good Shepherd Lutheran Church,** *2116 East Union, 325-2733,* a new Lutheran congregation, composed mostly of African Americans, was formed in 1951. The present building replaced an old frame church built for an earlier congregation of mainly Scandinavian descent. The church

*Claude Harris,
Seattle Fire Chief
since 1985.*

gives an annual scholarship in honor of early members **Edward** and
Marjorie Pitter. The church has a clothes closet, carols in nursing homes
and for shut-in church members at Christmas, and is raising funds for a
community center for neighborhood youth.

Copymaster Corporation Office, *2001 East Union,* (formerly the Pacific Northwest Bell Branch), was designed by architect **Leon Bridges** in
1966. Bridges began his firm in 1963 and became a partner with Edward
Burke in **Bridges/Burke Architects and Planners** in 1966. The firm opened
a branch office in Baltimore in 1970 which flourished. In 1972 the Bridges/
Burke partnership was dissolved, and Leon Bridges moved to Baltimore
where he opened a sole proprietorship which continues as TLBC, Inc. The
firm specializes in architectural design and planning, with capabilities of
construction management. Bridges has won many awards in recognition
of his work. In 1964 he won the Seattle Chapter of the A.I.A. "Home of the
Year" Award for the design of the home of Washington State Supreme Court
Judge **Charles Z.** and **Mrs. Ellie Smith.**

The **Gil Baker Building,** *northeast corner of 18th and Union,* bears the
name of its photographer owner and numbers among its tenants Co-Op
Books which carries an extensive inventory of books related to African
Americans and a small corner grocery owned by some of the new African
Americans from Ethiopia, an increasingly visible entrepreneurial group in
the city.

Along the south retaining wall of the T. T. **Minor School Playground,**
18th and Union, is a public art mural depicting jazz music-makers which
was painted by young neighborhood residents under the supervision of Don
Barrie in the mid-1980s.

The residence at *1474 21st Avenue* (∧) is still called the **Vrooman House**
by old-timers who remember its original owners. The house was constructed
by **Jennie** and **William Vrooman.** William was a much-decorated Spanish-

American War veteran, who was reported by the Seattle *Republican* newspaper in 1918 to have had an invitation from the Liberian government to train its army. While local legend says that she was a former Alaska madam, Jennie Vrooman was well known for her charity work, raising funds for churches and orphanages, arranging assistance for African American soldiers serving in France during World War I, oppressed brethren in the South, and the house-bound in the community. The Voormans operated a hotel in the International District which they sold in 1918.

The members of the Nation of Islam Study Group, #67, *1408 22nd Avenue, 860-8107*, have worshipped and studied together in Seattle since the early 1960s. For several years their small businesses dotted the Central Area. *This group sponsors twice-weekly lectures (Wednesday, 7:30pm and Sunday, 2pm) and a Friday study group, 7:30pm.*

Return to 23rd Avenue. Bus #48 travels the length of 23rd Avenue in the Central Area. Bus #4 travels along the northern and southern end of the street.

A small collection of paintings by local artists and prints from various places are shown at the Frame Gallery, *1106 23rd Avenue, 328-9424*, a shop of custom-made frames.

Inventions and agricultural experimentations by African Americans in Washington can be traced back to the plant experimentations and hybridizations of Thurston County's William Owen Bush as early as the 1870s. His present-day counterpart is Seattle's Roland Jefferson, recognized internationally as the authority on flowering cherry trees around the world, *P.O. Box 1094, Seattle, WA 98111-1094.*

Jefferson, a Howard University graduate who moved to Seattle in 1987, has documented varieties of cherry trees which grow in extreme climates to test the possibility of extending the southern and northern growing range in the United States. Botanical and horticultural institutions around the world use his system of record-keeping, and his solution to permanent labelling and plant identification is widely used. He was honored with a parade in Japan in 1989.

The "1105 Building" houses the optometry clinic of Mercer Island resident, Dr. Clarence Larry, Boeing engineer and optometrist, whose optical appliance invention was used in a space voyage in the 1970s.

Calneta Imports, formerly located at *1133 23rd Avenue* was a forerunner of the proliferating number of African import stores found in Seattle. It was begun in the late 1950s by Juanita Carter Russell, and a natural outgrowth of her work in assisting educational efforts in the former British East Africa colony. To support this effort she organized the Aid to Africa group which raised scholarship funds for African students. Russell was born in King County in 1907 to Gordon and Nella Carter who immigrated from Jamaica in 1903. Gordon Carter mined coal at Newcastle before he and his family moved to the Sea-Tac area about 1907. Nella Carter was the county's first professional African American social worker. One of their former homes is at 116 25th Avenue (∿). In the Seattle community during the Depression years she was known as "Mrs. Welfare" Carter. Juanita Russell, sponsored the African exhibition at the Seattle World's Fair.

For the next part of this tour you may want to travel by car or bus. Bus #3 East Cherry runs the length of Cherry Street.

Just beyond the northwest corner of 23rd Avenue and Cherry Street, *2212 East Cherry, 328-8132,* is the former location of **Daisy Boyetta's Garvey Bookstore,** the second bookstore operated in the county by an African American. (The first was that of Ethel Stone on Rainier Avenue in the 1910s.) Formerly this was an American Muslim restaurant. Now it is **Carolina's Corner.** Opened in 1992 by Ali Scego, this is the first business in King County established by a native of Somalia. In addition to sandwiches and ice cream, this store, and several others in the area, also sells African American-bottled Faygo soft drinks, and *kulet,* an Ethiopian red pepper sauce which contains many of the ingredients that enable—or embolden—American cooks to attempt home preparation of Ethiopian cuisine. The sauce is manufactured by Seattle-based **Setaté Foods,** *P.O. Box 22396, Seattle, WA 98122-0396, 720-6220.* Carolina's Corner is a clearinghouse for information relating to Somalia, and the relief effort. *(Somalia Relief Fund/Seattle; P.O. Box 22148; Seattle, WA 98122, 324-6600)*

The **Cherry Hill Baptist Church,** *700 22nd Avenue at East Cherry Street, 328-0894,* meets in the building occupied by the Grace Presbyterian Church from the late 1910s until their consolidation in the 1950s with Madrona Presbyterian Church at 32nd and Marion, formerly a White parish, which is now practically all black. This is one of the largest food bank distribution centers in the district. It is pastored by the **Rev. Jerry Laners,** who is preparing a dissertation on the history of African American churches in Washington. Retired pastor **Gil B. Lloyd,** past president and one of the founders of the **Black Friends of Yesler** (Douglass-Truth) **Library,** is a community *griot,* or keeper of the history, of the Seattle African American community.

The **Immaculate Conception Church,** *820 18th Avenue, 322-5970 ,* holds a gospel mass every Sunday which reflects the large African American congregation. The rector, the **Rev. Father John Cornelius,** is the first African American to head a Roman Catholic Parish in the Northwest. He has also taken the lead in the "One Church, One Child" movement to encourage the adoption of African American children by his example of adopting fifteen children.

One of the oldest self-help organizations in the county is the **Central Area Motivation Program (CAMP)**, *722 18th Avenue*, which was established in 1966. Under **Harold Whitehead**, its director, CAMP moved from an old Capitol Hill mansion with limited space for a burgeoning schedule of activities to this abandoned firehouse which, like many old Seattle firehouses, has undergone renovation and reuse. Initially the firehouse was planned as a Performing Arts Center which received its first funding through **PONCHO** (Patrons of Northwest Civic, Cultural and Charitable Organizations.) The actual work of conversion was performed by area youth under the direction of youth-program director, **Ernestene Givan** in 1967. Through the years CAMP has evolved to focus on social services. In its early days it held workshops in dance, visual arts, and a Friday Night Drop-In for young people. Artist **Paul Dusenbery** was director of the performing arts program. CAMP arranged free architectural services by the American Institute of Architects, sponsored a Central Area Department of Beautification, and published a monthly newspaper, *CAMP Trumpet*. In 1972 saxophonist and former University of Washington instructor **Joe Brazil** founded the **Brazil Academy of Music** here where it was housed until its closure in the mid-1980s.

A videotaped series of oral history interviews was a 1992 project of CAMP's innovative Rites of Passage program (ROPE) which provides mentoring and seeks to increase the self-esteem of low-income youth.

Since its inception, it has been headed by community activists. **Larry Gossett**, the present director, was one of the **Black Student Union** members at the University of Washington who occupied the office of the President to bring pressure to open hiring at the university to people of African descent, and expanded opportunities and services for minority, poor White and other disadvantaged students. Gossett was one of five Seattle community leaders who was invited to Japan in 1992 for a Multicultural Exchange and Education Tour to meet with high-ranking Japanese business and government officials. The group, accompanied by Seattle *Times* editorial columnist **Don Williamson**, was the first of seven from American cities to be invited. Gossett's immediate predecessor, **Eddie Rye, Jr.** was the prime mover of the long, but successful effort to rename Empire Way, in honor of Dr. Martin Luther King, Jr. In 1993 CAMP began sponsoring the *Underground Railroad, A Journey to Freedom* held in February. This cultural tour of Seattle's Central Area was developed by Rhonda Seals Hollingsworth, and first held in 1992.

Returning to 23rd Avenue via Cherry, turn right to explore 23rd Avenue southward to Jackson. An alternative is to continue eastward on Cherry Street. [See description of Cherry Street sites in this section following the Central Area Senior Center.]

Nurturing Mind, Body and Spirit

When **Merlie Evers Johnson** first saw the massive wall of the pool named for her late husband, Mississippi civil rights martyr, **Medgar Evers**, she exclaimed that it looked "strong, like a fortress." The **Medgar Evers Pool**, *500 23rd Avenue,* was built in 1970 and is operated by Seattle Parks and Recreation Department. Shortly after its opening it received an Honor Award from the U.S. Department of Housing and Urban Development during its fourth Biennial Design Awards Program. The ruined acrylic mural, *Omowale,* facing the street, was painted by neighborhood youth under the direction of **Curtis** and **Royal Alley-Barnes** and **Richard Sarto** in 1974. An eastward-facing section was painted under the direction of **Roy Sahali** and Rainier Waldman in the 1980s.

Directly across the street is the original **Ezell's Fried Chicken**, *501 23rd Avenue, 324-4141.* The fare is so tempting that television talk show host **Oprah Winfrey** relaxed her much-publicized diet after her staff flew Ezell's kitchen crew to Chicago to prepare chicken for her birthday in 1990. Although the primary offering is a succulent fried chicken, the restaurant also serves a "Creole style" chicken, fish, shrimp, homemade rolls that have few equals in Seattle, and potato salad. Especially good is the butter pound cake and the sweet potato pie. Catering and delivery services are available.

African Americans attended **Garfield High School**, *400 23rd Avenue,* when it was still in portables. In addition to a strong college preparatory program it has long had a strong arts focus. **George Lee**, a 1926 graduate began to syndicate his *Famous People* line drawings while still working for the Chicago post office. He has published his drawings in four books: *Interesting People, Inspiring African Americans, Worldwide Interesting People, and Interesting Athletes.* **Ernestine Anderson**, **Quincy Jones**, and **Jimi Hendrix**, among other talented, but less well-known folks, attended

Garfield. A bust of Hendrix may be seen in the library. The Garfield auditorium is now the **Quincy Jones Auditorium.**

Jones is a multi-talented musician whose albums, concerts, videos, films and television programs, have won twenty-five Grammy awards, more than any other individual in the history of the Grammys.

During the 1960s an outstanding magnet fine-arts program was offered at Garfield, with **Lorna Richards** teaching modern and ethnic dance and **Joe Brazil** teaching jazz, in addition to Dr. Stanley Chapple of the University of Washington music faculty teaching orchestra and William Cole leading the band. Garfield's jazz band, under the talented percussionist and director **Clarence Acox,** has won numerous regional competitions and played at the Montreux Jazz Festival in Switzerland in 1991.

The **Christian Methodist** denomination was organized as **Colored Methodists** in the southern United States in the 1860s. **Curry Temple Christian Methodist Episcopal Church,** *172 23rd Avenue, 325-9344.* originally called Bethel, was founded in 1949 under the guidance of the Rev. **H.Y.S. Sideboard.** It is presently pastored by the Rev. **Alex Pipper.**

The **Eritrean Community Center of Seattle and Its Vicinity,** *2400 East Spruce, 323-6627,* is a multi-purpose center. It serves as a clearinghouse for information about this growing population, has a community bulletin board with skill listings, offers church services, Eritrean language classes for children and ESL classes for adults. *The hall is available for rent. The Center is open Monday-Thursday, 3pm-10pm; Friday-Saturday, 10am-midnight.*

In addition to its **STARS** (Special Tutors for At Risk Students) tutoring program which assists more than five hundred children annually, **Central Area Youth Association,** *115 23rd Avenue, 322-6642,* has a strong sports program. Its Basketball Program had twenty-two teams and forty-two volunteer coaches in 1992. CAYA sponsors bingo to fund most of its activities, with some assistance from the city, state and federal governments. The renovation of this former bakery was designed by architect **Donald King.** Seattle school board member **Michael Preston** is the general manager of CAYA.

A playground at *119 23rd Avenue,* also designed by architect Donald King, is named after **Lawrence L. Brown,** a longtime supporter of CAYA. A 4-H Challenge Club with members from all over the city meets in the building next door south of CAYA. **John Little,** an early advocate of an African American academy for public school children in the Central Area, supervises the group. Central Area resident **Charles Huey** was another early advocate. (This academy is housed at the Sharples school complex on Beacon Hill.) Many of the 4-H Club projects are non-traditional, but one of the most popular activities in 1992 was their Rabbit Nutrition program. The club compiled a cookbook, *Favorite Ethnic Foods*, in 1992.

The **Douglass-Truth Library and African American Collection**, *23rd Avenue and Yesler Way, 684-4704*, contains the largest collection of African and African American material in the Northwest. The whole west wing is allocated to the African American collection, which includes a children's literature research collection tracing the portrayal of the African American experience in children's literature. In 1964 the Seattle Delta Upsilon Omega chapter of the national **Alpha Kappa Alpha Sorority** established their Library Project at Douglass-Truth. It is devoted to the historical and cultural contributions of African Americans to the nation's heritage. In 1991 the sorority added the seventeen-volume *Schomburg Collection of 19th Century Black Women Writers* to the collection.

The **Black Friends of Yesler**, which was organized in 1966, noting the lack of free meeting space in the Central Area, and the use of the library's basement for discarded book storage, began a successful campaign for renovation of the space for a meeting room. The room was renovated with Model City assistance, and dedicated in 1968 as the **Sam Smith Meeting Room**, in honor of Seattle's first African American city councilman. In 1975 the Friends, noting the ethnic and racial change in the community surrounding the library, launched a campaign for a name change that more closely reflected the library's constituents. The most popular two names submitted by community residents were **Frederick Douglass** and **Sojourner Truth**, thus the name change combined surnames of these two great African Americans.

Two murals in the library by Texas-born **Eddie Walker** portray Douglass and Truth. Prints of the portraits of great African Americans by Colorado painter **Clarence Shavers** hang in the room housing the African American Collection. The library has a slide presentation on the collection. The "soul pole" stands on the west lawn of the library. It was designed and carved in 1969 in a Model Cities Summer Arts Program by neighborhood students under the supervision of **Gregory X**, and was installed by Model Cities in 1973. A plaque states that it "depicts 400 years of the Black man in America." Gregory X was also art director of the Rotary Boys' and Girls' Club, *201 19th Avenue, 324-7317*, in the 1960s. *The library is open Monday-Wednesday, 1pm-9pm; Thursday, 10am-9pm; Saturday, 10am-6pm; Sunday, 1pm-5pm; closed Friday.*

The **Catholic Community Center** at the **Randolph Carter Center**, *23rd Avenue S. and Yesler*, was erected in 1975. It was originally named the Randolph Carter Industrial Workshop, for the civic leader and civil rights worker who pioneered the sheltered workshop concept in the Central Area. In 1968 he established a job-training agency for the physically and mentally-

"Soul Pole,"
depicting "400 years of
the Black in America,"
at the Douglass-Truth
Library.
(Don Mumford)

handicapped of Seattle which was called Seattle Central Area Industries, and after 1973, the Randolph Carter Center. The Randolph Carter Center commissioned Eddie Walker to paint the fifty-two panel acrylic, *Seattle Peoplescape*, which hangs in the building.

The Prince Hall Masons received a charter from English masons who were stationed in Boston in 1776. Since that time African Americans have formed lodges of various rites and charters among peoples of African descent throughout the world. The first masonic order of the York rite was established in King County in 1892. Some people say that the organization of Prince Hall lodges was spearheaded by Franklin miners who arrived as Masons in 1891. Until the 1980s most White lodges held African American lodges to be "illegitimate." Nevertheless, **Gideon Bailey** of Franklin and attorney **Con Rideout** of Seattle demanded, and received, recognition of the Prince Hall Masons in Washington by the White Grand Lodge of Washington in 1898. The Prince Hall lodge had several halls before purchase of this former Jewish temple, *306 24th Avenue, 322-9772*, in 1967. The hall may be rented for meetings and dinners.

You may end your tour here, or continue along Jackson Street, moving eastward from 23rd Avenue, or reverse the 12th Avenue tour at Jackson heading westward. The #14 bus serves the Jackson Street area.

The 23rd Plaza, *2301 South Jackson*, was developed by **Jimmy Sumler** in the early 1980s. This complex was planned to be the first part of a shopping center on both sides of Jackson.

Ron and **Iris Franklin** opened the **La Maison Bleu** gallery, *in 23rd Plaza, Suite 208, 322-8803*, in 1991. It features local African American artists, known and unknown, and a few from other states. The gallery provides framing, restoration, and a national art locating service and it will ship orders. La Maison Bleu provides a shuttle from Pioneer Square as part of that area's "First Thursday Gallery Walk." The primary focus here is on contemporary work, but older paintings and African art, such as antique Kuba cloth from Zaire, have been presented for display and sale on occasion.

Music Menu, (Beverly's) *Suite 205, 329-4888*, is one of two shops, and one of the oldest suppliers of records and tapes in the city. It has long supplied a wide-range of African American music to its loyal clientele.

A hidden treasure, which opened with the Plaza is the **City Shoe Store,** *Suite 204, 328-0463,* Its inventory includes a good sampling of narrow widths which are required by many African Americans.

The **Gideon-Matthews Garden,** *323 24th Avenue S. at Jackson Street,* opened in 1986, and is named in honor of staunch community advocates **Russell Gideon** and **Henrietta Matthews.** This forty-five unit complex is a Seattle Housing Authority building.

In the 1950s and '60s the storefront at *2515 South Jackson* was occupied by the (Marie) **Edwards Beauty School,** which served as a vocational school as well as informal support agency for former prison inmates, women returning to the work force and young women seeking skills for income with an eye towards establishing their own small business.

Perrino's Books, was here for several years in the 1980s. The store carried books and related items of African and African American subjects. Readings were held and occasional public access channel television programs were filmed at Perrino's.

Between the beginning of the first African American newspaper, the Seattle *Standard* in 1891, and 1901 there were seven newspapers functioning at some time during that decade, and there has been at least one paper functioning ever since. The Seattle *Republican*, begun in 1894 by Horace Roscoe Cayton published regular columns from the east King County mining towns of Franklin and Newcastle at the turn of the century. King County had four newspapers with an African American focus in 1992: the *FACTS*, the *Medium*, *2600 South Jackson Street*, *323-3070*, the Seattle *Skanner* and the *African American*. They are distributed country-wide on principal streets and in some shopping centers.

The Medium was begun in 1970 by Georgia-born Chris Bennett to "increase social and political awareness and then do something about it." This community newspaper has won the General Service Administration's Community Service award, and its editor and founder traveled with the UW football team as African American press representative and served as president of the National Association of African American Publishers. Bennett's sister, Constance Bennett Cameron, is editor of the paper.

Weekly circulation of this twenty page paper, which began with eight pages, was reported in 1990 to be 37,500 a week. The *Metro Homemaker*, a free weekly newspaper is also produced by this publishing company, in addition to weekly newspapers in Tacoma and Portland. Bennett operates radio stations in Seattle (KRIZ, 1420 AM) and Tacoma (KZIZ 1560 AM) and one station in Portland.

The Black Journalists Association of Seattle sponsors the Patricia Fisher scholarship Fund for local African American high school students, and encourages students to pursue careers in journalism. *Information: Neal T. Scarbrough at the Seattle Times, 466-2276 or 282-5101.*

Mark Wilson and Howard Ziegler opened Every Body Health and Fitness Center, *2609 South Jackson, 324-6062* , in 1991. The latest in body-building equipment is housed in an 1898 building, one of the oldest commercial buildings in this part of town, which the owners renovated to open the Central Area's first such amenity. Regular African aerobic dancing is offered here. Gospel (!) aerobics was introduced in 1992. The Everybody's Espresso bar offers fruit beverages and baked goods, and some of the best coffees in town.

The Flo Ware Park, *28th Avenue S. and South Jackson Street*, was named after petitions were signed by local residents in recognition of the volunteer services Florestine R. Ware rendered to the community. Ms. Ware was involved with foster care, the educational needs of Central Area youth, and nutrition for the elderly. She and her co-workers were able to obtain grants through the Model Cities Program to establish the county's first group home for youth. She also helped to acquire the present site of the Central Area Senior Center where she originated the idea of the lunch program for seniors.

King's Court, *2900 South King Street,* is one of the seven apartments designed and built by the Peck and Merriwether firm [see Madison, Route 2] in 1969.

The Seattle Association of Club Women purchased the residence at *161 30th Avenue (N)* in 1963, and sold it in 1989 because of an increasingly aging and decreasing membership. The Seattle Association is a member of the Washington State Association of Colored Women's Clubs which was formed in 1917. The first clubhouse owned by African American women was a Queen Anne style Victorian house which occupied the site just north of the restaurant at the northeast corner of 23rd and Union. It was purchased by the Sojourner Truth Club in 1919 with proceeds from a cookbook, and assistance from other chapters in the state.

At the Central Area Senior Center, *30th Avenue S. and South King Street,* a variety of classes are held for retired persons, from dance lessons to Bible study. This multi-purpose center serves the Central Area community beyond its natural constituents. Wedding receptions, anniversary dinners, and other activities are held by a cross-section of people who rent the facility.

Alternative Routes
To continue the exploration you may proceed west on Jackson from 23rd Avenue or reverse the last part of the 12th Avenue tour. Another alternative is to continue the exploration of Cherry Street by returning to 23rd Avenue and traveling north to reach Cherry Street. Turn right onto Cherry and head east.

After leaving 23rd Avenue, pause to view the Mural Art, on the dressing room at Garfield playfield which was painted by neighborhood children in a summer employment program in the mid-1980s.

If you pass by Dave and Bessie's Down Home Barbecue, *26th Avenue and East Cherry,* at the right time of the morning, you will see the smoke streaming from the traditional smoker in the yard which is used to produce the meat that received the "Best Barbecue at the Bite" award at the 1990 Bite of Seattle. You're bound to agree with the judges on this one.

In the early 1980s Catfish Corner, *2726 East Cherry at Martin Luther King Way, 323-4330*, was the home of the gargantuan, highly-acclaimed One Stop "Suicide Burger." Today Catfish Corner regularly offers outstanding southern favorites, such as mustard greens, hush puppies, beans and rice, and "Auntie's" peach cobbler in addition to their award-winning namesake. Gumbo is served on Wednesdays.

Across Martin Luther King Way is the **Girls Club of Puget Sound,** *708 MLK Way, 329-3310,* which bears the name of its founder, **Alvarita Little,** long an advocate for children and students. Ms. Little was an early member of the Foundation for International Understanding through Students, *543-0735 or 543-2100,* and has hosted numerous foreign students from throughout the world. She has received many awards and recognitions for her work in programs benefiting girls. There are two branches of the Girls Club, the other in West Seattle. Recreational and educational programs are offered at the club all year round, including a summer day camp. In 1987 **Crystal Mowatt** was named Girls Club of America's national winner of the Donna Brace Ogilvie Creative Writing for Poetry Award.

The *FACTS Newspaper, 2765 East Cherry, 324-0552,* is the oldest African American publication in the Northwest. It was begun by the late **Fitzgerald Beaver** in 1962. Shortly after coming to Seattle to operate a radio station, Beaver decided to start a newspaper. Beginning his weekly on a shoestring, he was reporter, advertising salesman, typesetter, photographer, and circulation director, and he never missed an issue.

The S.S. H.F. Alexander's waiter's crew, 1923. Harry Duvall, in dark suit, and James A. Roston formed the Colored Marine Employees Benevolent Association in 1923 to secure employment for African American men. (Robert Wright)

During the 1970s he published a Tacoma edition. The paper continues under the management of his widow, **Elizabeth Beaver**, and their family.

The YWCA branch now at *2820 East Cherry Street* was originally organized in 1917 by **Mrs. Corrine Carter** as the Phyllis Wheatley branch after the first African American poet. The first location of **East Cherry YWCA**, was in a converted house on 24th Avenue, which was later returned to its original function as a dwelling. The present structure was designed by Benjamin McAdoo in 1952.

You can smell the *injera*, the slightly fermented bread of Ethiopia, as you approach the building housing the **Assimba Ethiopian Cuisine Restaurant**, *2920 East Cherry, 322-1019*. A good sampling of vegetarian, beef and lamb dishes are served here. Accompanied by injera, of course. Traditional spiced (and aromatic) tea and coffee are available. **Messeret Tessema**, owner and cook, is a member of the **Ethiopian Community Center** committee which is seeking a permanent location.

Abba Haddis Gedey, administrator of the **Ethiopian Orthodox Amanuel Church**, ministers to the spiritual needs of the Ethiopian community and to all persons of the African Diaspora seeking a link to Africa in the ancient Christian tradition. *Address: Box 12043, Seattle, WA 98102; telephone: 323-0846 or 324-3362.*

Leschi
Head west on Cherry and turn southward at Martin Luther King

The initial impetus for development of the four acre **Powell Barnett Park**, *Martin Luther King Way, between East Alder and East Jefferson,* came in the early 1960s from the Leschi Improvement Council, which was joined by the Model Cities Program and the Central Area Motivation Program. It was named for Powell Barnett, a longtime Leschi activist, by Leschi Elementary School children. Barnett grew up in Roslyn, where he played on the baseball team and organized the Citizen's Band of Roslyn. He moved to Seattle about 1906 and organized the **10th Division Band** which played for soldiers who went to World War I from Seattle. After the war he organized the **Mount Zion Community Orchestra** which accompanied the choir and played in city parks in summer. He also organized the **African American Musicians' Union, #493**, and later headed the committee which brought about amalgamation of the African American and White unions. The trees in the park were contributed by CAMP, whose Beautification Project planted them and prepared the grounds for seeding with grass. The Model Cities Program was headed by **Walt Hundley** who later became the superintendent of the Seattle Department of Parks and Recreation.

You may want to visit **Peppi's Park,** at the end of Yesler. [See Capitol Hill]

The building at *820 Martin Luther King Way S.*, opened in 1972 as **Heritage House,** a restaurant-theater night club. This building occupying a 1.3 acre site, has undergone several changes of ownership, name and function since its original conception as a major entertainment center for Central Area organizations.

RAINIER VALLEY

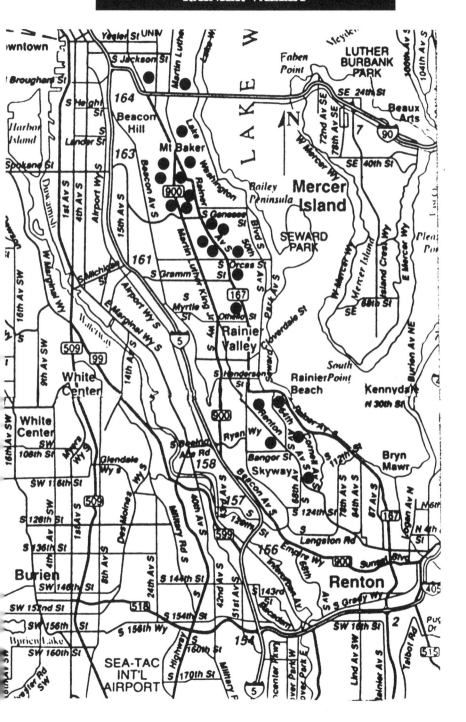

9.
Rainier Valley

Good View, Good Food

This area of the city is undergoing a quiet revitalization. The northern part of Rainier valley was once called "Garlic Gulch," referring to the presence of one of the largest Italian populations in the Northwest at the turn of the century. It has been home to a succession of ethnic and racial groups, beginning with the Germans, followed by Italians, African Americans and most recently, large numbers of Southeast Asian immigrants. The racial and cultural diversity of the valley is even greater than the Mt. Baker area. African American settlement throughout the area began in very small numbers around the turn of the century, and increased dramatically in the 1960s. Today they are one third of the population of Southeast Seattle, the second largest concentration of African Americans in the county after the Central Area.

Several small businesses are found here, as are many small churches. Some are located in the Columbia City Historic District, which is now on the City of Seattle's Landmark Register. Lumber from this area helped to rebuild Seattle after the Great Fire of 1889. African American businesses, artists, and architects are contributing to the growth and development of this part of the city.

Rainier Valley can be approached by traveling along 23rd Avenue South, Rainier Avenue, Martin Luther King Way, or westward on I-90 and then to the Rainier Avenue South exit. From I-5 from the south end of the county, use the Martin Luther King Way exit. The #7 Rainier bus makes frequent runs from Capitol Hill to downtown on Third Avenue beginning at Union and proceeding southward. The #48 bus travels from Ballard through the University District, along 23rd Avenue southward to Martin Luther King Way South.

One of the most exciting events held in the Rainier Valley is the annual **Pacific Northwest Black Community Festival** *at Judkins Park, between 23rd Avenue S.and 21st Avenue S. at South Judkins Street.*

Formerly known as the **Mardi Gras Festival**, the Black Community Festival takes place during the last weekend of the Seafair Festival. The

One of ten murals painted in the Mt. Baker tunnel by community youths in 1989.
(Bob Pickens, The People's Photo Studio)

Mardi Gras parade was begun in 1948 by the East Madison-East Union Commercial Club and expanded into a Community festival in 1952. The Festival parade, held the first Saturday of August, ends at this park. Michael Taylor, *P.O. Box 22867, Seattle, WA 98122, 723-9245,* is president of the Festival Association.

Continue eastward on Judkins to reach the I-90 pedestrian and bicycle tunnel through Mount Baker ridge, a good place to start viewing the emergence of public art in this area. Travelers from the south should depart MLK at South Judkins Street, turning right. At the end of the block, turn right again to approach the tunnel.

The ten murals inside the tunnel through the ridge were painted by twenty community youths mostly of African, Asian, Hispanic and Native American background. The work was sponsored by Seattle's **Summer Youth Employment Program** in cooperation with the State Department of Transportation, Washington State Arts Commission and other public and private agencies in 1989. The young artists were supervised by a team of professional artists, including muralist **Eddie Walker.**

Return to Martin Luther King Way. Continue southward.

The residence at *1742 Martin Luther King Way S.*, was owned by **Robert** and **Madeline Wright,** who led the struggle against discrimination in the city's golf clubs and associations which used the names of the city's golf courses. In 1958, the Park Department, after receiving complaints from members of the **Fir State Golf Club,** wrote the men's and women's clubs of Jefferson Park, West Seattle and Jackson Park Golf Clubs, notifying them that they would have to change their names or cease discriminating. Each club changed its name and continued rejecting African American applicants, while continuing to play at golf courses supported by the public. The rejection effectively barred African Americans from entering tournaments. After a formal complaint was filed with the Washington State Board Against Discrimination in 1959, the Wrights sued the city.

The Wrights' son, **Bill,** was National Public Links Champion in 1959, but met constant rejection. He was the number one player on the Franklin High School golf team in 1953, and says that his father, who began playing golf in 1926, was one of the finest golfers in the United States, but he was never allowed to play in tournaments. Theirs is a story of frustration and persistence.

For doctrinal reasons, the music at **Holgate Street Church of Christ,** *2600 South Holgate Street,* is always sung *a capella.* This church is home to the **Cross Connection,** a young adult singing ministry founded in 1972 which sings in prisons and nursing homes. The group has traveled throughout the nation, and has recorded five albums. Jimmy Hurd currently serves as the church's local evangelist.

The **Martin Luther King Memorial** is a good place to have a picnic in warm weather with a calming sound of the monument's splashing water in the background. [See Capitol Hill—Celebration and Remembrance]

Note the mural at the bus shelter underneath the pedestrian overpass at Rainier and Hanford Street painted by a multi-racial group of Franklin High School students under the guidance of Anabel Peña in 1991.

Andrew Bain, a Franklin High School student, was the 1991 winner of the high school Seventh Congressional District Arts Competition for his painting, *Locked in a Peaceful Unity.* In this competition, sponsored by Representative Jim McDermott, Bain's painting, part of a yearlong nationwide exhibit of students' work, was on display in the nation's Capitol in Washington, D.C.

Franklin High School is a south end anchor. [See Capitol Hill-Mt. Baker Tour]

No one source in the county lists every arts-related event, but both the *Seattle Arts,* publication of the Seattle Arts Commission *(312 First Avenue N., Seattle, WA 98109-4501, 684-7171, TDD 587-5500,)* and the *Arts,* published by the King County Arts Commission, *1115 Smith Tower, 506 Second Avenue, Seattle, WA 98104-2311*, provide a monthly calendar of events as well as arts exchange pages. Contact the commissions to be placed on the mailing lists. Heritage and cultural activities are announced in Community History, newsletter of the King County Historic Preservation Program. *For information contact Charles Payton, editor, at 1115 Smith Tower, 506 Second Avenue, Seattle, WA 98104, 296-8693 or 1-800-325-6165. The Pacific Northwest Ethnic News,* published by the Ethnic Heritage Council of the Pacific Northwest, *3123 Eastlake Avenue E., Seattle, WA 98102* has regular features on African American life.

The **Silver Fork Restaurant,** *3800 Rainier Avenue S., 721-5171,* is a convenient place to pause for good food at reasonable prices. Some of the best African American chefs eat here, as do construction workers. Breakfast is a popular meal, with an early bird special between 6:30 and 8:30am weekdays. A twenty percent senior citizen discount is offered on Tuesdays. *MasterCard or Visa accepted.*

While you're close by visit the **Jones Clavier Academy of Music,** *3847 Rainier Avenue South, 722-4500,* founded by Gracie Jones in 1974. This full line music store and studio provides instruction in drum, saxophone, guitar, piano and trumpet. Sheet music, as well as music books are available here. Should you want to try an instrument before buying one, you may rent one here.

Public funding has enabled schools to expose children to the work of professional artists through purchase of artwork as well as through working with artists in the schools. **Hawthorne Elementary School,** *4100 39th Avenue South,* boasts a painting by **Gwen Knight Lawrence** in its collection which was funded by the Washington State Arts Commission. Lawrence was born in Barbados and grew up in New York. Her work, in both public and private collections, has been exhibited in New York, California, and the Northwest.

Some of the children attending Hawthorne in the early years of the twentieth century were African American and lived in farm-like settings in the Rainier Valley. The Rainier Avenue Safeway store, *Rainier Avenue at Genesee,* occupies what for many years was the Burton family home. Myrtle Burton Giles, a 1927 Franklin High School graduate, once recalled, "We

*The Silver Fork Restaurant, a family-owned restaurant which
specializes in soul food. (Don Mumford)*

were raised where the Safeway is on Rainier. It was out in the country then...
outhouses, chickens, cows and horses." The area retained its rustic character until relatively recent times.

Nearby is one of the newer buildings in the area, the **Columbia Health
Center/Rainier Park Medical Center,** *4400 37th Avenue South,* which
opened in 1990. The entry displays a large soft sculpture assemblage by
Madrona area sculptor, **Monad Graves,** who is known for his whistles in
ceramic and other materials as well as for soft sculpture and apparel. The
artwork was dedicated on the first day of National Children's Health Week
in October of 1992. The warm quality of this hand-sewn sculpture appeals
to adults and children alike, and may be viewed during regular clinic hours.

The **Columbia Health Center** was established after **Claude Forward,**
who is sometimes called "the honorary mayor of Genesee," successfully
lobbied the city for funding for a community clinic. Forward, who played
an active role in the expansion of the Rainier Safeway store and improvement of the neighboring area, has operated **Claude's Color TV,** a television repair business at *4405 Rainier Avenue* since 1957. For his role in the
Safeway expansion Mayor Norman Rice declared January 27, 1992, the
day of the store's opening as "Claude Forward Day."

A few doors down **Chris' Lousiana Style Food,** *4421 Rainier Avenue
S.,* 725-2196, features such specialties as Cajun chicken, dirty rice,

jambalaya, and catfish. The buttermilk pie elicits raves. *Dining in and carry out service is available. Open Tuesday-Saturday.*

The Rainier Community Center and Playfield, *between Alaska, South Conover Way and South Oregon Street* is one of the most popular gathering places in the valley. The annual **Soul Fest** celebration, preceded by a parade in the Central Area, which is sponsored by the Seattle *Medium* newspaper, is held here the third weekend in July. *For information call The Medium, 323-3070.*

The Emerald City Tennis Association dates its formation from a Labor Day Picnic at the community center in 1989. It was formally organized January 31, 1990, and held its first meetings in **Mary's Kitchen** restaurant on Judkins Street. Since that time membership has grown to about eighty-five players, at all levels with a diverse range of careers. Players come from as far as Northgate and the Tacoma area. The group meets the second Saturday of the month at the Columbia Branch Library, has a monthly play party during the winter months, annual tennis tournaments at Seattle Tennis Center, and meets in an exchange visit with African American tennis players in Portland. The association is a member of the United States Tennis Association and the seventy-five year old (African) American Tennis Association. The Emerald City club, since 1990, has focused on reaching children through tennis and encouraging educational excellence. In 1991 it held its Summer Junior Development Program for thirty-one youths at the Rainier Community Center tennis courts. The program was funded by a seed grant from the U.S. Tennis Association. Membership includes a monthly newsletter. *ECTA president, George Monroe, 728-1925 or 448-0633, has additional information.*

A few professional African Americans lived or worked in Rainier Valley by 1916. During the 1970s, the **Odessa Brown Children's Clinic** became a showcase of periodontic care in the Northwest. This success was due to the work of **Michael B. Washington**, a graduate of the **Howard University School of Dentistry**. Dr. Washington and his wife, **Carol**, established the family dentistry clinic at *4543 Rainier Avenue South* in 1978.

Northwest African American fashion designers occasionally exhibit their talents in special shows. At G.K. Bradford's, *4824 Rainier Avenue, 723-2124,* it is possible to purchase clothing by **Adini** of Rhode Island and other custom designers. Men's clothing and accessories are also available here.

At the busy heart of the historic district is **Art Images Northwest**, *4869 Rainier Avenue South, 723-5144,* which began as a frame shop and print gallery on South Edmonds Street in 1987. It is a combination gallery, card shop (all occasions, African themes and Kwanza), and espresso bar. *Layaways are accepted, and mail orders are invited.*

The Landmark Café, *4868 Rainier, 760-1833*, one of the newest eateries opened by African Americans, specializes in Soul food as well as such Creole food as gumbo, oyster and shrimp loaves, Cajun fried chicken and pork grillades. The servings here are hefty; the rice and beans and the collard greens are some of the best in the Northwest. The café features "Late Nights" with live music on Fridays and Saturdays. *Open Monday-Saturday beginning at 8am.*

If it is too damp to eat outside, eat at the restaurant, then spend some time at the Little Record Mart South, *4200 South Othello.* The original Little Record Mart was opened in 1942. Come here to catch up on the latest music releases. If the weather is warm and dry and you prefer to eat outside, ask that the food be packed for carry-out, and head east on Ferdinand Street to the mini-park between *41st Avenue and 42nd Avenue S. and Americus Street* for a picnic.

This little park was designed and developed by architect **Denice Hunt** in the early 1980s for the Southeast Effective Development agency. Hunt, now the city's urban designer, has analyzed the impact of development on neighborhoods and the creation of land use plans and policies. She has developed proposals for the retention of open space in the city, and established guidelines for development in greenbelts and environmentally sensitive areas.

Return to Rainier Avenue and continue southward.

After their first clubhouse was razed for the new Bailey Gatzert School on Yesler Way, the **Royal Esquire Club** moved to *5016 Rainier Avenue, 723-2811.* Recreation and meals are available to members and their guests. The hall is available for rent. Organized in 1947 the Esquire Club sponsors a number of community outreach activities, and gave eighteen thousand dollars in scholarships to fifteen students in 1992. Live jazz and blues is featured every Sunday for members and their guests.

Next door to the Esquire Club is the Radical Women's Headquarters, a meeting hall and small store which carries titles on African American history and politics. During the year various issues relating to African Americans are examined through panels and lectures held here.

Church membership in the valley reflects the diversity of the community more often than in most churches in the county. The private funeral of the late rock guitarist, Jimi Hendrix, was held at one such church, the **Dunlap Baptist Church,** *8445 Rainier Avenue South,* on October 1, 1970.

If you're exploring the area on a weekend, enter the driveway of the **South Shore Middle School,** *8825 Rainier Avenue S.,* to view the mural painted by students in 1990. **Dr. John German,** principal at Southshore, began voluntary recruitment of African American students for the U.S. Naval Academy in 1990, recruiting three that year. He is now a Blue and Gold officer, or minority coordinator for recruitment in Washington State.

At Henderson Street, jog a few blocks west to Renton Avenue S.

Hats are still favored for churchgoing by African American women. Those women with a passion for hats may indulge their fancy at **BC&H,** *8821 Renton Avenue S., 725-1425,* a one-stop shop which also carries accessories and large size clothing.

Return to Henderson Street, driving eastward to reach Rainier Avenue.

The Rainier Beach Library, *9125 Rainier Avenue S.,* usually has a Black History exhibit during February. Poet and writer, **Carletta Wilson,** Adult Services librarian, is the library's liaison with the Rainier Beach Library Mural Project which is overseeing a mural on the library's eastern wall. The Southeast Seattle Arts Council is sponsor of the project which is scheduled for completion in 1993.

Across the street from the library is a small shopping mall where you will find the **Music Menu,** *9196 Rainier Avenue S., 725-7005,* which has been providing a wide selection of popular records and tapes for the past two decades.

Since the 1920s gospel music has enjoyed enormous popularity. Several small businesses in the county handle records and tapes and serve as clearinghouses of information about this accessible art form. **Highest Praise Music Shop,** *9252 57th Avenue S., 723- 2307,* stocks a wide range of gospel recordings of vocalists, solo and group, at reasonable prices. In 1992 it began its gospel television show on Cable Channel 29, featuring videos, Christian Dance and Theater, and discussions on the business of gospel entertainment.

In the early years of the 20th century women's clubs displayed their members' artistic work at their conventions, and occasionally at special women's church meetings. **Frances Baker,** whom the Seattle *Republican* praised in 1917 for her tastefully furnished home and her artistic abilities, was active in the Tacoma Women's Art Club's successful attempt to have an art and needlework display at the 1909 Alaska Yukon Pacific Exposition, Seattle's first world's fair. Her paintings and needlework won three awards at the fair. She and her husband, Hiram, moved to the house at *6003 South Roxbury* (N) following their move to Seattle in 1914.

You may end this tour here, continue to Renton by traveling south on Rainier Avenue, or heading north, cross Rainier to reach Seward Park Avenue S. At South Morgan Street, turn east and head to Lakeshore Drive S.

In spite of a racially-restrictive covenant imposed in 1926, some of the houses in this neighborhood, the Uplands, were designed by **Benjamin McAdoo** in the late 1950s and '60s for White residents who were happy to use his architectural expertise. However, when the neighbors learned that the house he designed in 1961 for construction at *6261 Lakeshore Drive South* (N) was for the African American physician John R. Henry and his family, a furor ensued for months. Petitions were circulated, and thousands of dollars were offered to the family to discourage them from moving into the house. It was only after the mayor sent a letter to each resident describing the professional credentials of the owners that the agitation finally abated.

This was the residence for twenty years of retired librarian **Mary Turner Henry** who produced a slide-tape series and booklet on Seattle landmarks named for African Americans, Asian Americans and Native Americans. The series won an Association of King County Historical Organizations award in 1986. **Neil Henry**, one of the four children who grew up in this house, received three Pulitzer Prize nominations for his investigative reporting for the Washington Post where he worked from 1978 to 1992, part of the time as Bureau Chief for Africa. He was appointed distinguished visiting professor at the University of California, Berkeley, in 1992.

Alternative Route

This tour may begin along Martin Luther King Jr. Way starting near the Franklin High School Playfield where Martin Luther King Jr. Way crosses Rainier Avenue.

Persons familiar with this area may use several east-west streets to integrate this part of the tour into the exploration of points along Rainier.

Those less familiar may take South Alaska, South Edmunds, or South Graham Streets to reach Rainier.

A few blocks south of the mural at the pedestrian overpass between Rainier and Martin Luther King Way at Hanford is the **Fir State Golf Club Clubhouse,** *3418 Martin Luther King Way South.* This is the headquarters of the oldest African American Golf Club in the Puget Sound area. Members play on local courses and in regional tournaments in the western states. The club was formed in 1947 by African Americans who wanted handicaps, tournament play and social activities at a time when they were routinely barred from membership in clubs at the three publicly-funded city golf courses. The King County Golf Association, sponsor of the Public Links Tournaments, accepted Fir State Club members. Some of the club's members, particularly **Robert and Madeline Wright,** with attorney **James McIver,** brought lawsuits that resulted in monumental changes in the use of public money to support racially-exclusive practices in golf in Seattle. Fir State's youth program provides instruction and tournament arrangements. *Contact FACTS newspaper sports columnist, Dave Mann, for additional information about the club.*

Between Martin Luther King and Columbian Way South, Alaska Street to Sears Drive, is the **Rainier Vista Garden Community,** home to students, refugees, and low-income residents. The late architect **Benjamin McAdoo** and his wife, Thelma, lived here in a two-bedroom apartment at *4602 Escallonia Court,* while he studied architecture at the University of Washington. After graduation and a brief stint of working for other architects he began his practice in the kitchen of this apartment in 1947.

The Rainier Vista Community Center at *4500 Martin Luther King Jr. Way South* offers a variety of activities, including art classes, sponsored by the Pacific Arts Center's Artsreach Program, the Rainier Rotary club and the City of Seattle. In 1989 children participating in the program sculpted a mural in clay which decorated the community center. In 1985, **Afua Harris** *(P.O. Box 66202, Seattle, WA 98166, 722-6602)* began **Adefua African Music and Dance Company,** which performs dances, Djembe drumming, and song, here in the gymnasium designed by former resident McAdoo.

There are numerous churches in the valley with a variety of styles of worship and outreach programs. Women, such as **Gwendolyn Townsend,** great, great granddaughter of the pioneer Harvey family, fifth generation Seattleite and wife of Pastor **Sam Townsend Sr.,** are often in the forefront of church-related activities. She is the executive director of **One Church, One Child Headquarters** at Greater Glory Church of God in Christ,

6419 Martin Luther King Jr. Way South, 723-6224, 1-800-88-CHILD, the 38th state program established in the nation. It bases its recruitment of adoptive parents on the premise that the adoption of one child by a family from each African American church would eliminate the need for children waiting for adoption.

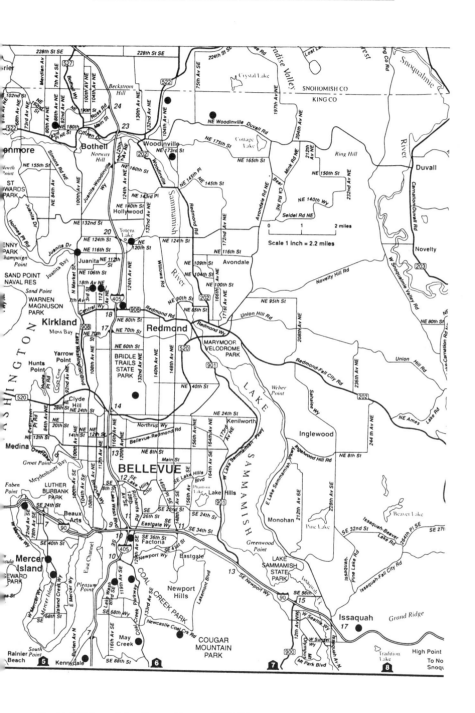

10.

Kenmore to Kennydale

Bridge to the Past, Roots to the Future

African Americans comprise less than one and a half percent of the population east of Lake Washington. Thus, sites related to their presence are far less numerous than in Seattle. Nevertheless, their long and varied association with certain areas provides interesting historical background to the present population which has increased to more than fifty-two hundred since 1980.

Both the Third Lake Washington Floating Bridge (I-90) leading from Seattle to Mercer Island, or the Albert V. Rosellini Floating Bridge, SR-520, formerly called the Evergreen Point Floating Bridge, are easily accessible from Seattle. These highways, I-405 and SR-522 (Lake City Way-Bothell Way NE), provide access to the area from all directions. Sites discussed in this section are in more or less northerly to southerly direction.

Traveling to the east side of the county is much easier these days than it was in 1938 when Gerald and Elizabeth Wells hired a taxi to drive around Lake Washington for their honeymoon trip. Around the time of the Wells' marriage Ora Avis Dennis received his Bachelor of Science degree in Civil Engineering from the University of Washington. He earned his Master of Science in Civil Engineering in 1940. Before he retired as a Supervising Bridge Engineer in 1971 he headed the design team for the elevated roadway on the SR-520 bridge. Dennis worked for the Department of Highways for twenty-six years.

Former Seattle architect Leon Bridges received the National Citation for Design Excellence in Community Architecture from the American Institute of Architects and the Federal Highway Administration in 1971 for his Seattle Interstate Highway I-90 Urban Design. Some of the construction work on the I-90 approaches was provided by Seaway Construction Co., headed by John and Barbara Pool. William Southern, who moved from Boston to Seattle in 1978, is the department's Public Affairs Officer for District One, which includes the I-90 project.

Kenmore

The Inglewood-Finn Hill area of Kenmore has three hundred and seven African American residents, the fifth largest concentration north of the I-520 bridge. This is a relatively new development. In 1980 there were just 23 African Americans in the area compared to 327 in 1990. Kenmore is home to 97. The combination of a large increase in available and affordable housing, what some newcomers perceive as a welcoming community, and good schools has encouraged, at least, in part, the growth in this area. Almost all of the African American residents commute to work in Seattle or, to a lesser degree, to the larger cities in the area.

Bothell

Bothell has 103 African Americans out of a total population of 11,342. In 1958 architect **Benjamin McAdoo** designed the house at *17823 88th NE* (*N*) where he and his family lived before selling it to move to Jamaica where McAdoo worked for the United States Agency for International

Barbara and John Pool, owners of Seaway Construction, prior to a concrete pour on the I-90 approach structure in 1988. (Michael Ziegler)

Development. The house was featured in the Rotogravure section of the Sunday Seattle *Times* in 1962. **Thelma McAdoo,** in the absence of her husband, participated in the ground-breaking of the Bothell **Southern Baptist Church,** *19527 140th Avenue NE,* which McAdoo designed in 1959. Several years after their return Thelma McAdoo, in 1980, wrote her charming little book, *Stories My Mother Told Me,* based on episodes from her mother's childhood in the Georgia Sea Islands in the 1800s.

Walter Backstrom, a family therapist and counselor, was the first African American to run for state office from an East Side city. In 1992 he ran for state legislator from the First District, which includes Bothell, garnering thirty-eight percent of the vote, the same percentage as his top Democratic opponent. The only Republican to run in the newly drawn district, Backstrom, a native of Watts in Los Angeles, is a former aide to Republican Congressman John Miller. He was rated "very good" by the King County Municipal League.

Woodinville

Gerald and **Bernice Morris Saulter** moved to the Lake Leota area of Woodinville near the Woodinville-Duvall Highway with their children in 1947 after a brief stay in Kirkland. The family spent the first summer in a tent while they cleared the ground, grubbed the stumps, dug a well, and began construction of the house that still stands on the 7.5 acres of land that the family purchased and still owns. Their son, Jerry, who grew up

there, is a former West Seattle resident. He was elected to the Seattle School Board in 1983, which he served as president in 1987. Jerry Saulter formerly worked for the federal government as an architect and is a former director of county executive administration.

An elderly couple, the Deans, preceded the Saulters to the area,

Ora Avis Dennis, head of the design team for the elevated roadway on the SR-520 bridge. (Bill Monroe, 1976)

but the number of African Americans continues to be very small, numbering just 155 of 23,650 in 1990. The shop addition to the Leota Jr. High School, 19301 168th was designed by McAdoo and his associates in 1979.

By the mid-1950s **McAdoo** had no shortage of commissions to design residential and small business structures in the county. His first commission for a church building came from a Seventh Day Adventist congregation in Oregon in 1947, followed by several from others of that denomination throughout the Northwest. Congregations of other denominations hired him for their churches as well. In 1955 he designed the Woodinville **Community United Methodist Church** at *17110 140th NE*.

At least one African American in Woodinville serves a larger population. The **Burger King** at *13514 NE 175th* is one of three franchises held by **Bruce Taylor,** who lives in Woodinville with his family. Taylor, a former stockbroker and San Francisco '49er football player, also operates two restaurants in Seattle. Between the three he employs about 120 people, making him the largest African American employer in King County.

African Americans worked as section hands on the railroad near Skykomish and Carnation. In 1920, for instance, a few workers could be seen near Skykomish, and **Isaiah** and **Lily Morgan** had nine boarders, who were section hands, living with them on Tolt Avenue in Carnation. **Joseph Moss** and his family lived there for awhile in the years prior to World War I.

Kirkland

In the early part of the century, visitors to what is now called Totem Lake may have noticed a shack reminiscent of those in primitive parts of Alaska. It was the home of **Israel I. Walker,** a graduate of North Carolina's **Johnson C. Smith College** who came to Seattle in the late 1880s. At the height of the Yukon gold rush Walker operated a grocery store in downtown Seattle at Second Avenue and Cherry Street from which he sold dried foods and other goods to northern-bound prospectors. Succumbing to the lure of gold himself in 1898 he went to the Yukon and remained there for the next ten years working as an independent paint contractor. Upon his return to Seattle, he operated a Jackson Street hotel until he retired to his Totem Lake property where he operated a berry farm. During Walker's day this area was called Firlock.

Three northern California transplants **Doug Martin, Robert Oatis** and **Keith Bowen,** friends since elementary school, operated restaurants and catering businesses in California, Miami and Chicago before moving to Bellevue. Their **Juanita Beach Broiler,** *9714 NE Juanita Drive, 820-8544,* serves food ranging from hamburgers to prime rib, and has a dance floor and bar. A live band plays the Top 40 on Friday and Saturday nights. The increasingly popular Sunday Jam Session begins about 6:45pm and is open to any musician who wants to sit in. The music varies with the players. Bring your own instrument.

Recalling Kirkland when the downtown consisted of one main street, **Maxine Pitter Haynes** described joyful summer days she and her sisters spent at the farm of **Anne Bellinger Turner** during the 1920s: " 'Auntie' Turner was a friend of our family. She had cows and chickens, and an outhouse; no electricity. She had lamps, and every morning we'd clean the chimneys. We used to go into town at night, clinging to each other, to attend the tent revival...going down the road, swinging the lantern. I can remember churning in an old square, wooden churn and she'd go to town to sell the butter. We would pick fruit and berries, and she would make ice cream with the boiled custard. I can close my eyes and see those two wooden picnic tables." The Turner farm was near what is now the Kirkland Jr. High School, *430 18th Avenue.*

Kirkland's African American population increased from 121 to 603 between 1980 and 1990, a dramatic increase over the three or four families residing there in the 1930s. The Wilkins family, in-laws of **Juanita Warfield Wilkins Proctor,** moved there in 1919. Mrs. Proctor's daughter, **Jacqueline Wilkins,** was the first child of African descent born in the Kirkland Hospital. Mrs. Proctor recalled living conditions when she lived there during the 1930s, before the "modern" era: "...when we got married, we went to Kirkland. We had fruit trees, chickens and turkeys...plenty to eat out there, but, oh! No city conveniences! Lamp lights, outside toilets–really country out there. We used to hear that ferry blow its whistle coming into Kirkland, and we would rush to make it there to catch it [for Seattle]....No bridge in those days. We used to love that ferry ride!"

During the Great Depression, **Frank Wilkins,** Jacqueline's father, often drove the eastern ranges of the county in a 1918 Ford with wooden wheels buying up surplus vegetables from farmers in Carnation, Kent, and Auburn which he then sold to downtown Seattle restaurants. The Wilkins farm was across the street from the Turner farm. Part of the playground of Kirkland Jr. High School occupies the site of the Wilkins' former home. Some members of the Wilkins family still live in Kirkland.

Kirkland was the home of **Willetta Riddle Gayton** in her retirement years. Born in Nooksack in 1909, she attended school in Bellingham and received her B.A. from the University of Washington in 1939 and her Bachelor of Library Science eight years later, the second African American to do so at the UW. Ms. Gayton was the first African American librarian in the Seattle Public Schools.

In 1972, she and several others attended a dinner party hosted by **Letcher** and **Arline Yarbrough,** Kirkland residents since 1950. Arline Yarbrough proposed a reunion picnic which resulted in the formation of **Relatives of Old Time Seattleites (ROOTS),** an organization of African Americans who were in the Seattle area prior to World War II. Their annual picnic is held at Seattle's Gasworks Park in early September. The Yarbrough's are the parents of Letcher, Jr. ("Jim") Yarbrough, photographer and writer, also of Kirkland, who was Deputy Executive Secretary of the Washington State Centennial Commission.

Just off of the Highway 405 interchange at NE 72nd is a Park and Ride lot occupying two blocks. Part of the lot and part of the residential area *between NE 68th and NE 69th and 117th and 118th NE in the Bridle Tree #2 Replat* is on the land purchased in the countryside by **Allen Deans** in 1891. Deans, an inveterate purchaser of real estate, was operating an employment office with T. C. Collins on Jackson Street in Seattle at the time of the Seattle fire in June of 1889. He and Collins operated a Seattle waterfront restaurant at the turn of the century.

Benjamin McAdoo designed the house at *2827 134th NE,* which was a Home of the Month selection in 1960.

The Antioch Bible Church was organized in 1986 by former Seattle Seahawks linebacker Ken Hutcherson and two other pastors. The congregation of about 1300 people of various races meets Sunday mornings in the gymnasium of the Seventh-Day Adventist Church school. African Americans, some of them professional athletes, are included in its diverse membership.

Redmond

Except for a few prisoners in the Willow Road county stockade, few African Americans lived in Redmond before the 1920s. However, their's is a much different story today. In 1990 when the population numbered 472, Redmond was one of the few places in the country where the average household income of African Americans exceeded that of White Americans. Many are employed at Microsoft or other near-by hi-tech industries. **Blacks at Microsoft** consists of about 80 members who are mostly eastside residents. Headed by Phoenix, Arizona native **Ron Douglass,** the group publishes **The BAM! Voice,** a monthly newsletter which features book, restaurant and movie reviews, welcomes to new employees, and a travel column. In the past the group has assisted the company in recruitment, and observance of the Martin Luther King holiday. Paintings by Seattle artists **Barbara**

Thomas, Gwen Knight Lawrence and **Phillip Lewis** are in the Microsoft Corporation's collection.

SAFE (Seattle African Americans for Excellence) at Allstate Insurance was organized in 1991 as a support group which encourages hiring retention and advancement of the company's African American employees. It serves as a resource and communication link for the company and attempts to identify a pool of potential employees. SAFE presents speakers and holds a special cultural celebration in February. **Maurice Scott** is the coordinator of the group.

Medina

For nearly two decades **John Woodson**, an elderly gardener, was a familiar sight as he made his way from his small cottage on Medina Avenue to the yards and gardens of villagers from the latter years of World War I through the 'thirties. **Nettie** and **Walter Rhodes** moved from their home in Seattle's Georgetown to the village to work in service there during the late 'teens and 'twenties. Seattle resident, **Charles Lewis** recalled, "They [the Rhodes] were great friends of my grandmother. I would go over with them on weekends . Medina in those years was very rural, lots of woods, dirt roads.... There were a few [White] families with estates or summer homes. I used to ride the horse, or walk around looking for garter snakes. I was walking down the road one time, and a grouse flew up, wings whirring, and scared the pants off me. The Rhodes owned an acre there. Our family wanted to buy it when they decided to move to California, but my family thought it was too hard to get to." The Rhodes were registered voters in Medina precinct during the 1920s.

Older residents of the county may remember the **Wake Robin Inn** [see page 146] between Medina and Kirkland which was operated by the **Cunninghams** and **Jameses** during the 1920s. Besides stock raising and farming this was probably the earliest African American enterprise on the east side. Featuring chicken as the specialty of the house, with steak offered, as well, the kitchen was supplied in season with fresh vegetables from the large garden of one of the owners' brothers. Older African American men worked as waiters, but **Hayward Roberts** remembers, "They were famous for their chicken. We (Garfield High School students) were glad to take the Medina ferry over there and someone would pick us up in a truck and take us to the restaurant. We'd wash dishes til late at night–five dollars a night."

Ruth Childs Watson was the first African American public school teacher east of Lake Washington. She began teaching at Medina Elementary School in 1957, prior to becoming an English teacher at Bellevue High School in 1961.

Bellevue

While Bellevue's African American population is relatively new, many Seattleites have been familiar with the area for nearly one hundred years. During the turn of the century Bellevue was the favored site of the annual August picnic of the Fraternal Order of Hawks which was a mutual benefit society. Taking the ferry from Leschi Park, picnickers began leaving Seattle by nine o'clock in the morning to enjoy a full day of dancing, baseball, listening to band music, and eating a sumptuous lunch. Some persons returned to Seattle as late as eleven o'clock in the evening, hastily alighting from the boat in a mad scramble to catch the last street car from the dock.

Lewis and Ernestine Chatman moved to the eastside in the early part of 1942. She recalled, "Our post office was Kirkland, the phone exchange was Redmond, and the children were always in the Bellevue schools. We were just below the line between Kirkland and Bellevue. There was one other Black family, the Donaldsons, down the street from us. They lived on five acres, we had ten. It's multiple housing all along there now." Mrs. Chatman's explanation for their move from Seattle has a familiar ring. "My husband just wanted to get out of the city," she said.

At least three major exhibitions on African American and African art have been held at the Bellevue Art Museum, *Bellevue Square, 454-6021, 454-3322*. Works by Florence Baker-Wood, metal designer who specializes in wearable art, and painter Barbara Thomas have been exhibited in occasional shows. Its 1989 retrospective exhibition of the paintings and sculpture of James Washington, Jr. inspired Patricia Gayton to work for an education program and packet which was largely funded by her and her husband, Phillip Gayton. A handsome catalogue, *Spirit in the Stone*, written by Dr. Paul Karlstrom with photographs by renowned Seattle photographer Joseph Scaylea, accompanied the exhibition.

The National Council of Negro Women sponsored exhibits and cultural events at Bellevue Square in celebration of Black History Month during the 1980s. Bellevue resident LaVerne Hall coordinated and provided leadership for these activities. Her daughter, Mahji' s, *"T" is for "Terrific," Mahji's ABC's*, (Open Hand) a book in English and Spanish, was published in 1987 when she was nine years old .

The work of Seattle resident Sam Cameron is part of an increasingly developed cityscape. As an associate of McKinley Architects, he was part of the design team for One Bellevue Center, and Rainier Bank Plaza at 777 108th NE.

The African American population in the city almost doubled from 1980 to 1990, increasing from 1,066 to 1,939 out of a total population of 86,874.

In 1990 a group of Bellevue and Redmond women organized a chapter of the international **Delta Sigma Theta Sorority**, the first chapter in the county of an African American sorority east of Lake Washington. That same year Bellevue Community College academic advisor and parent Chequita Williams-Cox was one of the founders of a group of parents of diverse racial backgrounds who formed "Concerned Citizens Caring" to encourage eastside parental involvement in education.

Mag Mallory began teaching at the college and formed the Genesis Group Consultants in 1986, two years after she moved to Seattle to work as a marketing associate with Metro-Municipality of Metropolitan Seattle (Metro). She is head of the marketing program at Bellevue Community College, and was elected 1990 president of Women Plus Business, a nonprofit organization promoting business and professional women.

African American businesses in Bellevue include a mortgage company, bridal salon, body salon, consignment shop, wardrobe shopping service and

Israel I. Walker's cabin at Totem Lake in 1938.
(King County Archives)

a consulting service. Sports-minded persons and collectors will be interested in one of the newer businesses.

Silver commemorative sports medallions bearing the likenesses of famous athletes is the brainchild and product of **Blanton Simmons** who with his wife, Ginny, and sculptor Max Karst are partners in the *Great West Mint, P.O. Box 40389, Bellevue, WA, 462-9424.* Local baseball players **Ken Griffey, Sr.** and **Ken Griffey, Jr.** are some of the latest athletes featured in their "Silver Signature Series" of collectors' medallions. Others include **Ken Easley, Patrick Ewing** and **Isiah Thomas.**

The non-White population of Bellevue's public schools increased from three percent in 1976 to more than twenty-three percent in 1992, with four percent being African American. When **Donald Phelps** completed his cadet teaching at Enatai Elementary School in the latter part of 1960, he was hired to teach at Robinswood Elementary School. In 1963 Phelps, whose mother, **Louise Gayton Phelps Adams,** attended the old Hazelwood School before World War I, became Robinswood's principal and the Bellevue Public School District's first African American principal. A few years earlier **Harrison Caldwell** was appointed principal in Seattle, becoming the state's first African American principal. After four years Phelps became principal at Bellevue Junior High School before becoming executive assistant to the president and director of personnel at Bellevue Community College where he authored the first college accreditation report. In 1970 he and his wife, **Shirley Norris Phelps,** built the house at *12835 NE 36th* (∧) in the Compton Green area. (Former Seattle Sonics basketball player-coach who now coaches the Cleveland Cavaliers, **Lenny Wilkins** and his wife, **Marilyn,** built a house there about the same time.)

In 1976 Phelps became interim superintendent of Lake Washington School District, #414 at Kirkland. He also served in the federal government and was director of executive administration of King County from 1977 to 1980. Phelps became president of Seattle Central Community College in 1980, and chancellor of Seattle Community Colleges four years later. In 1988 he was chosen to head the Los Angeles Community College District, the largest two-year college district in the country.

A name increasingly familiar to King County residents is that of **Norward Joseph Brooks,** who was appointed to complete the term of the late county assessor, Bruce Holland, following his sudden death in 1992. Brooks and his wife, **Violet,** moved to the house at *12512 SE 56th Street* in Newport Hills (∧) in 1963 and remained there until his election to office as Seattle Comptroller in 1986. He came to Washington as a missile specialist and second lieutenant in the army assigned to the Cougar Mountain Nike base. Because of discrimination by banks, developers, realtors, and neighbors, the family was unable to purchase property east of the lake. After his unit was put on fifteen-minute alert Brooks slept at the base. Later, through the efforts of a volunteer group and the Seattle Urban League, Brooks was able to move to Bellevue by having a White person purchase a house and then sell it to him. Ted Kenney, *Eastside Week* reporter, stated in a 1991 article that opposition of the community club to the Brookses' presence was ameliorated by the pastor of the Newport Hills Presbyterian Church, and the Brookses soon felt comfortable in their new neighborhood. Mr. Brooks was appointed by Governor Dan Evans, and later, Governor Spellman, as director of the Washington State Employment Security Division. Brooks ran for state treasurer in 1972.

Parents of African American Students at Tyee Middle School and Newport Hills High School was organized in 1992 when forty parents joined together in an attempt to encourage and strengthen academic performance of students and social support among African American parents. *Information may be obtained from Janet Batiste, 643-5608.* This group was preceded by the **Black Parent Group** of the early 1980s whose thirty to forty members were parents of students in all the Bellevue schools.

Newport Hills residents **Pauline Hill** and **Sherilyn Jordan** published a biography of 1913 Howard University graduate and **Delta Sigma Theta Sorority** founder, **Bertha Pitts Campbell**, in 1981. **Ralph Hayes**, after retiring from teaching history at Newport High School after eighteen years, wrote the *Centennial Tribute to Black Pioneers* (Bon Marche) in 1988.

In Factoria Square at *3846 124th Avenue SE*, The Rib Rack specialized in barbecue and its traditional accompaniments after it was opened in 1990 by Bellevue residents **Doug Martin**, **Robert Oatis** and **Keith Bowen**. The restaurant also offered catering and delivery services. Due to highway construction it closed in 1992. Black History Month activities were presented at Factoria Square by the National Council of Negro Women in the 1980s.

Mercer Island

Some of Mercer Island's three hundred African Americans are well known in the county for their achievements in a variety of areas. For the most part their careers are centered off the island.

One of the most prominent residents was Tacoma native **Roberta Spencer Byrd Barr**, the first African American woman principal of a Seattle high school. Barr, teacher and elementary school librarian, was moderator of a public affairs interview program on KCTS public television in the mid-1960s which was later broadcast from KING television. Barr was a storyteller for the KCTS "Let's Imagine" storytelling series, and for King County Library system. She served a five year term on the Washington State

Board Against Discrimination, and was active in the integration of Seattle schools. Barr starred in **Lorraine Hansberry's** *Raisin in the Sun,* a 1961 production of the Cirque Theater in Seattle, and in the 1966 revision of the play. She was chosen "Woman of Achievement" by the Seattle Quota Club and honored by the Matrix Table in 1967. In 1968 she became vice-principal of Franklin High School, and principal of Seattle's Lincoln High School in 1978. Barr retired upon the closing of Seattle's Lincoln High School. She shared the house at *4224 West Mercer Way* (∿) with her late husband, **Albert Barr.**

Mona Bailey is district Assistant Superintendent of the Seattle Public Schools. Bailey has also served as president of the national African American Delta Sigma Theta sorority. **Dr. Clarence Larry,** Boeing engineer, optometrist, and inventor of an optical appliance used in a space exploration lives on Mercer Island. And it was here that **Galen Marie Motin,** the only African American ever chosen queen of the Seafair, lived with her father, **James Motin,** also a Boeing engineer and her schoolteacher mother, **June Motin,** her younger sister and brother. The **LINKS,** an African American women's social and benefit club, had chosen her as princess when she was selected. Queen Galen was an honor student at Mercer Island High School and at Washington State University where she studied graphic design and advertising.

The **Matthews** moved to Mercer Island in 1964. **Meredith Matthews,** an executive in the YMCA began his career in Ohio in 1937 and came to Seattle in 1957, where he served as director of the East Madison YMCA. His fund-raising effort led to the erection of the present building. He served as associate executive of the Pacific Northwest Area Council of YMCAs from 1965 to 1971, when he was appointed regional executive of the Pacific Northwest region of YMCAs. He served on the King County Board of Appeals and Equalization. In 1966 **Henrietta Matthews** initiated a high school completion program for unwed mothers at the East Cherry branch YWCA, where she was executive director. Young women of all races and economic backgrounds from all over the city attended. Ms. Matthews is the only African American to receive the Bishop's Cross from the Episcopal bishop of the Diocese of Olympia. Except for a few years, when the Matthews lived in California, they spent the rest of their lives at the house at *3737 77th SE* (∿).

Linda Brown, a resident of Mercer Island since she and her family moved there from Seattle in 1974, became the first African American in modern times to operate a business on the island when she opened her "Essentially You" day spa at *2525 SE 24th, Suite 180, 236-5666,* in 1988.

Benjamin McAdoo designed the house at *4148 Boulevard Place,* which was selected as a Home of the Month by the American Institute of Architects and Seattle Times in 1954, the first year the awards were given.

The Gaytons at Hazelwood

The Hazelwood country place of John and Magnolia Scott Gayton, grandparents of Phillip Gayton and Donald Phelps, was a favored gathering site of the county's small African American middle class during the early years of the century. In his autobiography *Long, Old Road,* (Trident Press) **Horace Cayton, Jr.** provides a cameo description of one such gathering there. For a while Hazelwood became a year round residence for the Gaytons, who moved back to Seattle during the latter years of World War I. The late Louise Gayton Adams recalled in a 1976 interview: "We had four or five acres of land, just a block from the water, and it was up on the hill. My father commuted to Seattle every morning and he came home every evening on the little launch. I started to school at five years old and attended this little country school for five years. I walked about a mile and a half every morning and afternoon with neighbor children." Ms. Adams

Hazelwood School, about 1912.
Louise Gayton on left.

attended the one-room Hazelwood school before the 1915 construction of the "new" East Side schoolhouse. Due to the passage of years and the development of Hazelwood, Ms. Adams was not sure of the exact location of her family's home. County records up to 1920 do not list the Gaytons in transactions or ownership transfers that would pinpoint the location of the property. *The general location of Hazelwood is between Lake Washington on the west, 120th on the north in Bellevue, and SW 76th on the south.*

Newcastle

African Americans began employment at Newcastle, one of the state's earliest coal mines, a few weeks after the arrival in May of 1891 of about seven hundred miners and their families at the Franklin mines. While many were of southern birth, most of them came directly from Iowa, Missouri, and Illinois to Washington. Others came from within the state. Marcus Harding of Georgetown, Guyana, found his way there after jumping ship in 1903, and working briefly in Seattle. He was one of a few thousand who spent part of their lives working in one of Washington's most important early-day industries. Ultimately his children moved to Seattle, where some still live.

The nature of the work, including physical conditions of the mine which were affected by floods, lethal gases, rock falls and fires, as well as strikes, promoted a somewhat transient way of life, with miners and their families moving from mine to mine on both sides of the Cascades. Recollections of miners' children presently living in the county include their families' associations with such places as Coal Creek, Ravensdale, Newcastle, and Franklin in King County and Roslyn, Ronald, and Cle Elum in Kittitas County in central Washington.

African Americans remained in the two King County mining towns in large numbers for about ten years. During that time they served as constables and school board members, and were active in Repulican politics. Shortly after their arrival they formed churches and clubs. A contemporary newspaper reports that eight women "in the presence of the church and a great company of others" were baptized in the church's first baptismal rite in Coal Creek in January of 1894. The Colored Baptist Association of Washington State was formed at the Newcastle church in 1900. In the mid-90s they began leaving the mines to take up homesteads in the Yakima Valley. After the much-publicized gold strikes in the Klondike in 1898 coal miners joined the caravan. Those remaining until about 1900 either moved to other towns and cities or sought land in King County, principally in the Kennydale area. Exhibits, hikes and tours of the old town site are held annually on the first Sunday in June as part of the "Return to Newcastle" celebration sponsored by the Newcastle Historical Society, Issaquah Alps Club, *P.O. Box 351, Issaquah, WA 98027, 328-0480*, and the King County Parks Department, *296-4232 or 296-4281*. There is a parking fee.

Then, as now, mining coal was one of the most hazardous of occupations, as indicated by interments of miners, some as young as fourteen years old, in the old Newcastle cemetery which is under the auspices of the Newcastle Historical Society. The grave is on the National Register of Historic Places and the King County Landmarks Register.

To reach the cemetery on your own from Renton, take bus # 114 or the NE Sunset Highway to The "Duvall" Road to Coal Creek Parkway; make a right turn to 133rd remaining on it until you reach SE 72nd (which becomes SE 69th Way) and travel to 129th. The cemetery is across the street from Lake Boren. Bus travelers should call Metro for information. The cemetery will be locked but may be visited by calling Newcastle Historical Society members Milton Swanson, 1-206- 255-6996, or Oliver Rouse, 1-206-255-7381.

Coal Creek miners, about 1895.
(Renton Historical Society)

Kennydale

Several of the miners bought or rented small farms near Kennydale ranging from five to twenty acres, and by the first world war this was a flourishing small community. Some continued to work at Franklin or neighboring mines, keeping large gardens from which they sold surplus produce to their fellow workers.

A small church built on the land that **Henry Jones** gave to the community around 1907, and was later demolished, was the center of the social life of this community. The **Renton Full Gospel Pentacostal Church,** *1015 North 29th Street in Kennydale, 226-7411, (Exit 6 via I-90, turn left to 30th Street)* which draws its one hundred members from all over the county, serves a similar function.

Magadalena Threet Thompson published *Seattle/The Pride of Our Hearts Today,* her chapbook of poems, while she lived in Kennydale in the early 1950s. She was brought to Franklin in 1891 as a child. Some of the descendants of the mining families still live in the area.

Issaquah
As principal architect of Environmental Works in 1987 **Donald I. King** provided preliminary planning and design for the twenty-eight unit duplex home project in the *4100 block of 244th Place SE* in the cul-de-sac of this Klahanie residential subdivision. Called Lake Park Town Homes, the fourteen duplex houses complement the existing single-family homes in the neighborhood.

Snoqualmie
Ski Acres, at Snoqualmie, is the favored skiing and instruction site of the **Four Seasons North West** club, an organization which promotes year

*Lake Park Townhomes were planned and designed
by Donald I. King for Environmental Works in 1987.*

around leisure activities with an emphasis on skiing. The club estimates that there are 1,200 regular African American skiers in King County, and projects a ten percent growth rate per year. Former UW football player, **Joe Jones,** organized FSNW in 1973, the same year as the **National Brotherhood of Skiers,** an African American group, was founded. FSNW is a charter member of the national organization. Beginning with fifteen youths in 1981 the **FSNW Youth Ski Academy** was established to provide intensive training to enhance the proficiency of young skiers. *For information, contact Joe Jones, 323-9329.*

You may end the tour here, or proceed to Renton. Should you prefer to go to Maple Valley and points further south instead, turn east on South Second Street in Renton and follow the signs.

An alternative would be to head northward on Sunset Boulevard to Edmonds Avenue NE or Aberdeen Avenue NE to reach the Kennydale area, continuing on to explore the east side in reverse order of that outlined here. King County Metro Transit operates throughout the area.

Note:
Wake Robin Inn has been identified as being on *108th SE* in Bellevue.

RENTON TO ENUMCLAW

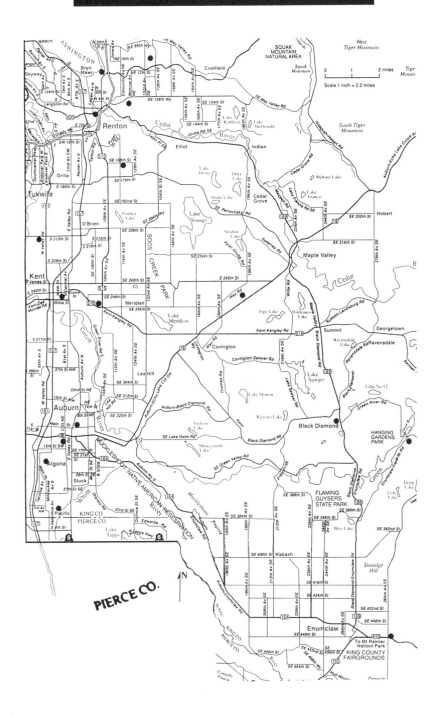

11.
Renton to Enumclaw

Where Coal Was King

African American farmers and mine workers came to Renton in the 1890s. Of the early residents of the area, Lucretia and Milton Roy remained there longest. When they first purchased property in Bryn Mawr shortly after its platting in 1891, they were the only African American family living there. The Roys moved from Seattle where they had operated a hotel and were founders and faithful members of the African Methodist Episcopal Church.

The African American population increased slowly up until World War II. By 1990 2,462 were living in the Bryn Mawr-Skyway area. One pre-War resident, Irene Grayson, is now over one hundred years old.

Alfred and Irene Grayson were born in Oklahoma, Indian Territory in the late 1880s. They came to Seattle with their children in 1913, residing there until they purchased ten acres near Cemetery Road (now Fourth Avenue) in 1929. They logged off the land and, using the logs, erected their first home, a log cabin which has since burned. The purchase of this land on the eve of the Great Depression was the salvation of the Graysons. The family planted a large garden from which came the produce Mrs. Grayson peddled in Seattle from the back of her car to earn the family's income during those difficult years.

During the 1940s, in the wake of the wartime boom in employment, several hundred African Americans moved to Renton where many were hired as defense plant workers. Most of them lived in governmental housing in the Renton Highlands area. At the beginning of his architecture studies at the UW Benjamin McAdoo and his family lived here. An annual picnic held the second Saturday in August at the Gene Coulon Memorial Beach Park, *1201 Lake Washington Boulevard*, was conceived in 1974 by the late Bernice Barfield and her son, John, to foster the renewal of friendship among the wartime residents, and fellowship with the later arrivals. Her daughter, Beverly Barfield Lucas, *228-9437*, continues the coordination of the event.

The population has continued to grow. While most of the newer residents are not famous, Renton is the home of former Seattle Mariner baseball player and children's advocate, Harold Reynolds. Rainier Beach High

School art teacher and painter **Elmore Williams**, lives here. His work has been exhibited in the Seattle Urban League's Annual Art Show, Bellevue and Renton Art Shows, at Green River Community College, and the Museum of History and Industry. He had a one man show in Renton in the mid-1980s. **Gary White**, a Seattle Times employee who lives in Renton, published a book of poems, *Living Testimony: A Tribute to the Black Woman*, in 1992. Renton is also the home of **Gloria McCoy-Waller**, publisher of *Ethnic-American Experience Magazine*, *P.O. Box 1235*, *Renton, WA 98057*, and the *Sea-Tac Community Newspaper*.

Today more than six percent of Renton's 41,668 residents are African Americans, many of them young families. About one-third of Renton High School's students are African American. **The Black Parents Association** (**Stanley Friendship**, president, *235-4579)* is one of the strongest African American organizations in Renton. It was formed in 1984 to address the needs of their children in the city's schools. Each year the group sponsors four scholarships, a Family Night in February with a program and potluck dinner, and participates in the annual **Martin Luther King Day March,** which starts in Skyway in Renton, and meets southward-marching Seattleites at Rainier Beach High School.

The increase in population gave rise to the establishment of churches. Prior to church organization, an informal group met at the Graysons for some years. **The Martin Luther King, Jr. Memorial Baptist Church,** *13611 SE 116th*, *255-1446*, was organized in 1978, and moved into its new building in 1990. It is actively engaged with the greater community through its food bank, contributions to the Renton food bank, its volunteers with Union Gospel Mission in Seattle, and its home and jail visitations. The membership numbers about three hundred. It is pastored by the **Rev. Dr. Leon C. Jones.**

Parish Overseer, the **Rev. Mattie Bass** of **The Seed of Abraham Pentecostal Church,** *246 North Wells Street at Third Street*, traveled with other church members to a World Camp meeting in Zimbabwe in 1991 where she was one of several foreign guest speakers. The church is pastored by the **Rev. Habakkuk Evans.**

In the last few decades, African Americans have branched into a variety of callings, some of them unique, sometimes of a brief life span. One of these, **Afro-Link Software,** was established at Renton. It was the first electronic bulletin-board system in the nation aimed at increasing African American awareness of the potential of computers for African and African American culture. The bulletin board, called **CPTime Online,** a tongue-in-cheek reference to the reputed casual regard for time held by some African Americans, was founded by **Kamal and Angela Mansour** who moved to Renton from Boston in 1989. The board offered information on technical, political, historical and educational subjects. The company also offered clip art for graphics and desktop publishing and Black history games and programs. Evidence of the past in southeast King County may be discerned from photographs of African American coal miners in the King County mines of the late 19th and early 20th century. Such photographs are part of the collection of the **Renton Historical Society and Museum,** *235 Mill Avenue S., 255-2330.* Duplicates may be ordered. Appointments for research are advised, as the museum is staffed by volunteers.

Many African Americans are buried at **Greenwood Cemetery,** *350 Monroe Avenue NE, 255-1511,* including world famous guitarist, **Jimi Hendrix,** who revolutionized rock music with his electric guitar. Hendrix is buried in the Azalea Section, near the sundial.

To reach the grave drive about one half block from the cemetery office parking lot to the first right turn. Continue to the next junction, then turn left. Continue driving straight to reach the sundial. Bus #107 from the downtown Seattle bus tunnel, or from downtown Renton stops near the graveyard.

The grass is usually trampled from the feet of large numbers of visitors from all over the world who visit the grave every day. The cemetery office which is open from 8am to 4:30pm every day likes to have visitors to Hendrix's grave sign the register.

A substantial part of the increase of Renton's African Americans continues to come from migration. In 1991 another former Boston resident, painter and craftswoman **Pat Lacey** opened **Routes to Roots,** *16932 116th Avenue SE, Cascade Center, 235-7446.* Formerly, the store featured Nigerian textiles, jewelry and wall hangings. Lacey has since switched her focus to concentrate on exhibiting and selling the work of African American artists from around the United States.

Maple Valley

African Americans have tried farming at Maple Valley since the 19th century. Most of their efforts were of short duration. Beginning in the 1910s a few city residents in search of additional land to farm or to retreat to during the summers bought land here. By 1920 **Susan Johnson,** an eighty-four year old widow, was the only African American farmer in Maple Valley.

In Kentucky and other southern states in the 19th century African Americans were the primary trainers of race horses. Today they are barely associated with the industry. King County is one of the few places in the country where they can still be found as both owners and trainers of race horses, as well as the more traditional groomers.

Herman Cotton was one of three trainers at Long Acres in 1971 (the others being former UW football player **Junior Coffey** and a **Mr. Jones** of

Jacqueline and Herman Cotton (second and third from left)
with Fair Court, winner of race in August 1968.
(4-Footed Productions)

Seattle's East Madison District) when he and his wife, Jacqueline, to avoid the expense of boarding horses, bought five acres between Wax Road and state highway 18 at Maple Valley. Cotton was a city boy from Birmingham, Alabama, but upon leaving his job at Seattle City Light, and going to work at Long Acres, he fell in love with thoroughbred horses. Cotton entered the business when he traveled to Kentucky to buy two race horses for himself and East Madison restaurateur, Lum Honeysuckle, his first partner. Wilbur Morgan, who owned the Mardi Gras Grill on East Madison was also a partner for a few years. Over the years the Cottons owned from two to five horses at a time, and Cotton trained winners. By September of 1980 Cotton, as a two-horse trainer, had won a third of the twelve races he entered that season. He died in 1987. His widow, Jacqueline, had not previously worked with the horses, and, upon his death, sold all the stock except one brood mare. Since 1991 she has become more involved with horses. The farm, located in what is now called Jacqueline Meadows, was sold upon her husband's death and has been platted for the construction of seventeen homes.

In 1992 local businessman Nona Brazier was elected King County Republican Committee chair, the first African American in the Northwest to hold such a position.

Black Diamond

Over the years African Americans in Black Diamond have rarely exceeded more than five individuals at one time. The 1990 census lists two.

Perhaps the "largest" family to ever live there was that of Booker and Francis Kirk and their children Willis Coleman, Raymond Leonard and Sandra Roston. The Kirks purchased a twenty-three acre farm on the Black Diamond-Auburn Road in the west end, or Morgansville section, of the town from Mr. Kirk's brother, Peter, and his wife, Cecile, in 1946. They remained on the land until 1987. Their house and one acre were sold in 1978, but the remaining twenty-two acres have been divided between the Kirk children. Willis is a home builder and developer. Raymond is a plumber, and Sandra has been a faculty member and administrator at Shoreline Community College since 1969.

In the photography collection of the Black Diamond Historical Society Museum, (*Thursdays, 9am-4pm, Saturday and Sunday 12m-3pm or contact Mr. and Mrs. Carl Steiert, 206-886-1168 to visit by appointment*) are images of African American miners who first came to the Franklin coal mines, two miles east of Black Diamond, in 1891. This is the best place in the county, if not the state, to get a view of a simulated early 20th century coal mine, and tools and implements of the industry.

Franklin

The arrival of about seven hundred miners in Franklin, accompanied by their families, brought the number of African Americans in the county to about one thousand by the middle of 1891. Some of the dreams of 19th century African Americans were realized in Franklin long before they were in Seattle which, since the turn of the century, has had the largest population.

From the beginning of their stay in Franklin, African Americans served as constables and deputies. **Gideon Bailey**, Civil War veteran and recruiter of soldiers for the famed Massachusetts 54th Regiment, was one of two African American justices of the peace appointed in Washington in 1894, among the earliest in the Pacific Northwest. The miners came in May and by October of 1891 two of them were elected members of the school

The Minisee family at their Franklin home, about 1907. (Courtesy Ralph Minisee)

Black Heritage Society Tour to Black Diamond Museum, 1985.
Left to right: Don Mumford, Timothy Frederick, Community Museum Advisor Charles
Payton, Esther Mumford, Green River Community College professor John Hanscomb,
Carl Steiert, Don Mason, Don Davenport, and Ralph Hayes. (Tollefson)

board. It was 1969 before the first African American, **Alfred Cowles,** was elected to the Seattle school board.

The population in Franklin was composed of people who came from all parts of the country, and some of them were of foreign origin. They had served on both sides in the Civil War, although those in Confederate ranks had been forced to do so. Their political affiliations were, like most African Americans of the day, with the Republican Party, but there were a few people identified as Democrats in some of the elections of the 'nineties. The state's largest branch of the **Afro-American League,** a national civil rights group, was in Franklin. Under the state organization's first president, **Gideon Bailey,** the league advocated migration from repressive southern states to the new state of Washington, and monitored a variety of civil rights issues.

The Coal Miner Who Came West (Moore Enterprises, 1982) the autobiography of **Ernest Moore,** grandson and son of Franklin miners, who also mined, describes part of the coal mining experience. Moore has also developed a video documenting the African American experience at

Franklin.

Excavation of the abandoned Franklin townsite was a state Centennial Celebration project of the archaeology class at the Green River Community College. A written report was compiled and may be available from the college bookstore. **Professor Gerald Hedlund** coordinated the project. **Professor John Hanscomb** is the author of *Company Coal Town/Franklin and the Oregon Improvement Company, 1880-1896,* a study of the corporation and mine and the importation of African American miners. The professors may be contacted by calling the GRCC Archaeology Department, *telephone (206) 833-9111 ext. 389; from Seattle, 464-6133.* The college received an Association of King County Historical Organizatons award for its Franklin History project in 1992.

Enumclaw

In addition to the pigs, pies and potatoes at the annual King County Fair *(1-206-296-8888, 1-206-825-7777)* are featured appearances by such famous entertainers as **Charley Pride** and **Ben Vereen.** The fair is held the second week in July.

The most direct route from several points in the northern part of the county is via the Maple Valley Highway, traveling southeast out of Renton. From Seattle the trip takes about forty minutes by car.

From the southern end of the county, the Auburn-Enumclaw Road leads directly there. Public transportation is available by "King County Fair Special" buses which leave the Auburn Park-and-Ride at 15th and A Streets NE. King County Metro (553-3000) has fare and time schedules.

In 1990 there were sixteen African Americans in Enumclaw. Architect **Benjamin McAdoo** designed the dressing room at **Enumclaw Field House** on *284th SE,* north of the fairgrounds. The **Mud Mountain Dam** is a few miles south of Enumclaw. **Horace Foxall,** architect for the Army Corps of Engineers, designed the Corps' modular administration building, *30521 Mud Mountain Road,* in 1984.

Bibliographic Note

This bibliographic note is a selective compilation of the sources drawn upon for information in reconstructing and interpreting the past and describing present-day activities and sites.

The literature on African Americans in the county is limited and needs to be expanded. Several unpublished sources and archival collections were useful: Sara E. Dawson, "A Brief History of Ebenezer A. M. E. Church," (n.d.); Don Sherwood History Files, 1884-1970, Seattle Park Department, City of Seattle Municipal Files; Board of Park Commissioner's Minutes, City of Seattle Municipal Archives; and the papers of Powell Barnett and James Roston, Jr. in the Manuscripts Division, University of Washington Library.

Quotes and descriptions, as well as background information, were extracted from the oral history transcripts of Ora Avis Dennis, Dr. Giles Graves, Eugene Coleman, Fern Johnson Proctor, Edward Johnson, Sara Oliver Jackson, Priscilla Maunder Kirk, Muriel Maxwell Pollard, Juanita Warfield Proctor, Fred Woodson, and Elizabeth Dean Wells. These transcripts are in the Oral History collection of the Washington State Archives in Olympia. Transcripts of architects Horace Foxall, Jerry Saulter and Mel Streeter in the Black Heritage Society collection were particularly valuable. I was able to incorporate personal information from my own interviews of Roberta Byrd Barr, Dr. Blanche Lavizzo, Jacob Lawrence and Dr. Millie Bown Russell.

Resumes and project lists of Leon Bridges, Horace Foxall, Denice Johnson Hunt, Donald I. King, Benjamin F. McAdoo and Streeter/Dermanis and Associates are the best guides to the contributions of African American architects to the county's built environment. I have included additional information on McAdoo's career in the forthcoming A.A.A. publication Seattle *"Masterbuilders:" A Guide to Seattle's Architects* (1993)

For eyewitness accounts of African American life in the county from 1889 to the 1960s see Emma J. Ray, *Twice Bought, Twice Ransomed* (Chicago, 1926) and *Seven Stars and Orion/Reflections of the Past* (Seattle, 1985), a collection of oral histories which I edited. My first book *Seattle's Black Victorians/1852 to 1901* (Seattle, 1980) provides background information on the 19th century population.

Weekly editions of community newspapers–the *FACTS*, the Seattle *Medium*, the Seattle *Skanner*–and the Seattle *Times* were surveyed during the course of the writing of the book. Most editions of the early 20th century years of the Seattle *Republican* are still available and extremely valuable for researching the period from 1901 to 1917. Ed Pitter and Peter DeBow's *Who's Who? Among the Colored People of Washington State* is an old but still valuable compilation of biographies of late 19th and early 20th century residents. Junius Rochester's Seattle *Weekly* article on Doc Hamilton is a lively addition to the cast of colorful Seattle characters. With the exception of a few scattered articles on African Americans east of Lake Washington they have been rarely mentioned. Ted Kenney's *Eastside Week* article (1991) adds measurably to the subject.

Gervais Reed and Jo Nilsson's *Art in Seattle's Public Places/Five Urban Walking Tours* (1977) have been succeeded by more recent guides, but are still valuable in their detailed descriptions of the art and architecture of the city.